work, Love, SUFFERING, death

work, Love, SUFFERING, & death

A Jewish/Psychological Perspective

through Logotherapy

REUVEN P. BULKA
WITH A FOREWORD BY VIKTOR E. FRANKL

JASON ARONSON INC.
Northvale, New Jersey
Jerusalem

Copyright © 1979, 1998 by Reuven P. Bulka

10 9 8 7 6 5 4 3 2 1

All rights reserved. Printed in the United States of America. No part of this book may be used or reproduced in any manner whatsoever without written permission from Jason Aronson Inc. except in the case of brief quotations in reviews for inclusion in a magazine, newspaper, or broadcast.

Library of Congress Cataloging-in-Publication Data
Bulka, Reuven P.
    [Quest for ultimate meaning]
        Work, love, suffering, and death: a Jewish/psychological perspective through logotherapy / by Reuven P. Bulka.
        p.   cm.
        Previously published: The quest for ultimate meaning. New York : Philosophical Library, 1979.
        Includes bibliographical references.
        ISBN 0-7657-9960-X
        1. Logotherapy. 2. Judaism and psychology. I. Title.
RC489.L6B85 1997
616.89'14—dc21   97-30946

Manufactured in the United States of America. Jason Aronson Inc. offers books and cassettes. For information and catalog write to Jason Aronson Inc., 230 Livingston Street, Northvale, New Jersey 07647.

In memory of
the recently departed grandparents of
our children-in-law:

Henry (Don Zvi Aryeh) Hook
and Abraham (Avraham) Tabachnik
Grandparents of Chani and Shmuel Bulka

and

Sidney (Yeshaye) and Lilly (Rochel Leah) Speiser
Grandparents of Moshe and Yocheved Shonok

May their progeny follow in their wonderful ways

IN MEMORIUM

VIKTOR EMIL FRANKL, M.D., Ph.D.

(1905–1997)

Survivor of Four Concentration Camps
Insightful Analyst of What Ails Us
Courageous Critic of a Self-Centered Universe
Inspired Teacher to the World
Transmitter of Meaning to Those in Search
Enhancer of All Our Lives

His "Past Is Our Future"

CONTENTS

Foreword, *by Viktor E. Frankl* — xiii
Introduction — xv
Acknowledgments — xvii

SECTION 1
THE TECHNIQUES OF LOGOTHERAPY

Prelude — 3

1 Is Logotherapy Authoritarian? — 5

2 Paradoxical Intention and De-Reflection: Return to Naturalness — 21

SECTION 2
LOGOTHERAPY AND RELIGION

Prelude — 33

3 The Ecumenical Ingredient in Logotherapy — 35

4 Is Logotherapy a Spiritual Therapy? — 45

SECTION 3
LOGOTHERAPY AND JUDAISM

Prelude — 61

5 Logotherapy: Its Relevance for Jewish Thought — 63

6	Logotherapy and Talmudic Judaism	73
7	Logotherapy and Judaism — Some Philosophical Comparisons	83

SECTION 4
CONFRONTING DEATH

Prelude   103

8	Reflections on Past and Future	105
9	Death in Life—Talmudic and Logotherapeutic Affirmations	111

SECTION 5
LIVING WITH TRAGEDY

Prelude   123

10	Logotherapy and the Talmud on Suffering: Clinical and Meta-clinical Perspectives	125
11	Logotherapy as a Response to the Holocaust	138

SECTION 6
THE DAILY LIFESTYLE
LOVE AND LABOR

Prelude   149

12	The Meaning of Love	151
13	The Work Situation: Logotherapeutic and Talmudic Perspectives	164

SECTION 7
TIMELESS TRUTH

Prelude   177

14 Hasidism and Logotherapy: Encounter
    Through Anthology   179

Conclusion   197

References   199
Footnotes   205

FOREWORD

Ever since logotherapy was introduced to the academic community and the public at large by my first books, it has attracted the attention not only of psychiatrists and psychologists but also of religionists and theologians. The more the books, which originally had been published in German, were translated later on into other languages (today, they are available in eighteen tongues), the more the echo was fed back from a variety of Christian denominations as well as Eastern religions. Jewish responses were relatively rare, but only until Dr. Reuven P. Bulka started writing on his comparative studies between logotherapy and Judaism. As may be seen from the bibliography on logotherapy, he has continued writing on this subject more than any other scholar, and thanks to this volume, the pertinent articles are made easily available to anyone who is interested in the matter.

Dr. Bulka did not intend to present a systematic work. Rather the contrary is true. Each chapter focuses on a particular phase, or aspect, of the system called logotherapy. What is even more important and should be kept in mind by the reader, is the fact that some areas in which logotherapy has been applied even most successfully, have been discussed by Dr. Bulka only sketchily and only in layman's language; that is, logotherapy as a "theory and therapy of neurosis" (to use the title of one of my books which is not available in English). But as is the case also with respect to other specific topics, the reader really interested in them may find, after being *introduced* to logotherapy by Dr. Bulka, the respective information in my own books, last but not least, in *The Unheard Cry For Meaning*. Incidentally, the preceding volume, *The Unconscious God*, propounds my view on the borderline problems between "psychotherapy and theology" (to quote its subtitle).

May I now be allowed to share a personal reminiscence. When I arrived in Auschwitz one of the few things I still had with me because I wanted to keep it as long as possible (but finally had, of course, to leave it there together with the scarce rest of my possessions), was a small piece of a mosaic that stemmed from an ancient synagogue of Jerusalem. Its age might have been about two millennia. I had bought it many years before in Vienna and treasured it in order to cement it into the cornerstone of my house if I ever should possess a house of my own.

I never did (and frankly speaking, don't give a damn for owning one). But I did recover the mosaic. In a way. Because a mosaic—this is exactly what I see in the work of Dr. Bulka: Single pieces each of which forms part of the whole picture. And it is precisely the fragmentary quality—or should I say, the humility?—which makes for the beauty of a mosaic.

This feature corresponds, on the part of Dr. Bulka, to the modesty with which he explicates his comparative studies in this "mosaicesque" book. Dealing with logotherapy as evaluated in particular from the viewpoint of Judaism, it may aptly be defined as a *mosaic* mosaic.

VIKTOR E. FRANKL

INTRODUCTION

Work, love, suffering, and death—these are the major components of a complete life. And they are the primary focus of this book.

But you will not find herein a conventional treatment of these life contingencies. Instead, work, life, suffering, and death are studied from the vantage point of a unique psychological system known as Logotherapy, and within the Judaic framework.

What is Logotherapy? Logotherapy is a school of psychology that is the product of the mind and heart of the late Dr. Viktor E. Frankl. It concerns itself with all the dimensions of human existence, even as Frankl himself combined expertise in neurosurgery, psychotherapy, philosophy, and even theology.

Logotherapy has been described as healing through meaning. We normally think of therapy as being concerned with the immediate moment, and so it should be. But it remained for Frankl and his logotherapeutic teachings to show clearly that the meaning of the moment cannot and should not be divorced from ultimate meaning. Logotherapy is concerned, at once, with the immediate and the ultimate, with the present and the future.

Before exploring the four major life components—death, suffering, love and work, we introduce the reader to Logotherapy, and to the common links between Logotherapy and Judaism.

The first section describes how Logotherapy works as a clinical tool and offers some insights into two unique logotherapeutic techniques, "paradoxical intention" and "de-reflection."

The second section concentrates on how Logotherapy relates to religion, philosophically and clinically, with the third section developing the common ground between Logotherapy and Judaism. The implications of these relationships are also explored in these sections.

We then proceed to the more intricate studies. How to deal with the fact of death and the fleetingness of time is the subject of section four, with the fifth section projecting Logotherapy's approach to the various dimensions of suffering.

Love and labor are the concerns of section six, with many logotherapeutic insights offered for the marriage and work situations. Often, Talmudic counterparts to the logotherapeutic viewpoints are given.

Section seven, the final section, rounds off logotherapeutic wisdom in its major facets and shows how it parallels hasidic wisdom.

In the process of presenting these insights, the book includes features such as helping techniques, developing proper attitudes, building healthy philosophies, and affirming unconditional meaning. All this is particularly timely in an age plagued with the malaise deriving from lack of meaning, purpose, and direction.

There is some overlap in this book, a repetition of some ideas and concepts. The decision to allow for this overlap, the variations on the same theme, is based on the realization that each article is an entity in itself. Too much of the spirit of each chapter would be lost in the chopping process.

I like to think of these repetitions, like the repetitive themes in music, as a symphony of and on life. Symphonies, it is well known, grow on the individual as the themes are introduced and embellished. In music, familiarity breeds inspiration and repetition enhances appreciation.

Hopefully, this volume will do the same for the life symphony that includes work and love, and yes, even suffering and death.

REUVEN P. BULKA

ACKNOWLEDGEMENTS

In any publication, there is always more than one author. The thoughts projected by the official author reflect the many ideas gleaned from absorbing thoughts in the world of letters. This volume is no exception, and gratitude is expressed to the hidden partners whose ideas are at work in this book.

Specifically for this volume, there is one person for whom my indebtedness cannot remain hidden, if indeed it could even be camouflaged. I speak of the late Professor Viktor E. Frankl, the founder of Logotherapy. My relationship with him over the past three decades had been most meaningful and inspirational. The time we spent together showed that the warmth and all-embracingness of his books reflect the warmth and all-embracingness that was his very being.

Logotherapy is not abstract thinking. It is real and authentic, as any encounter with Frankl would prove. This book is a small way of acknowledging the many vistas of meaning Frankl has opened up for so many.

Arthur Kurzweil of Jason Aronson, Inc., a gentleman and scholar, has been, as always, most helpful with his insights and useful suggestions, not to speak of his encouraging the publication of this book. To Arthur and his gracious staff go my profound thanks.

Gratitude is extended to the publishers of the following journals for granting permission to reprint my articles which originally appeared in their publications. They are listed in the order they appear in this book.

Journal of Humanistic Psychology for "Is Logotherapy Authoritarian?" (18:4, Fall 1978), and the responses of Rollo May and Viktor Frankl which appeared in that volume.

Journal of Ecumenical Studies for "The Ecumenical Ingredient in Logotherapy" (11:1, 1974).

Association of Mental Health Clergy Forum for "Is Logotherapy a Spiritual Therapy?" (30:2, Jan. 1978).

Jewish Life for "Logotherapy: Its Relevance for Jewish Thought" (11:2–3, Fall–Winter 1978), under the title "Logotherapy—A Step Beyond Freud: Its Relevance for Jewish Thought."

Journal of Religion and Health for "Logotherapy and Talmudic Judaism" (14:4, 1975).

Tradition for "Logotherapy and Judaism—Some Philosophical Comparisons" (12:3–4, Winter–Spring 1972); and for "Logotherapy as a Response to the Holocaust" (15:1–2, Spring–Summer 1975).

The Jewish Spectator for "Reflections on Past and Future" (Sept. 1972), under the title "Logotherapy and Judaism."

Humanitas: Journal of the Institute of Man for "Death in Life—Talmudic and Logotherapeutic Affirmations" (10:1, 1974).

Journal of Psychology and Judaism for "Logotherapy and the Talmud on Suffering: Clinical and Meta-Clinical Perspectives" (2:1, Fall 1977); "The Work Situation: Logotherapeutic and Talmudic Perspectives" (2:2, Spring 1978); and "Hasidism and Logotherapy: Encounter Through Anthology" (3:1, Fall 1978).

These articles first appeared many years ago, but maintain their timeliness to this day. That should be no surprise, since Judaism itself has stood the test of time and has withstood the challenges of time, and Logotherapy is firmly anchored in timeless and timely tradition.

SECTION 1

THE TECHNIQUES OF LOGOTHERAPY

PRELUDE

Logotherapy is a unique approach to the clinical situation. Unfortunately, it has been misunderstood by some who have imputed to it authoritarian tendencies. *Chapter One* is a response to one such charge leveled by Rollo May. In refuting May's allegations, a conceptual framework for how logotherapy addresses the clinical situation is developed. The context and content of logotherapeutic thinking and technique are projected.

The article which forms *Chapter One* elicited a response from May and a counter response from Frankl. These too are included in the presentation.

Chapter Two offers an insight into the specific techniques developed by logotherapy, "paradoxical intention" and "de-reflection." These techniques emanate from logotherapy's view of the person. They mobilize human capacities rather than manipulating the person. They are employed in the clinic but can be used by everyone for the large and small challenges of everyday. Both "paradoxical intention" and "de-reflection" emphasize the freely willed control of attitudes toward one's predicament. They are, in fact, a return to naturalness.

Chapter One

IS LOGOTHERAPY AUTHORITARIAN?

Rollo May is considered the founder of the existential psychotherapy movement in America. The book, *Existence,* which he edited together with Ernest Angel and Henri F. Ellenberger[1] and to which he contributed two major articles, represents the first real attempt to bring the thought and therapy of the European existentialists to America.

Against this background, it would be instructive to examine a statement May makes about logotherapy, the healing-through-meaning philosophy and psychotherapy of Viktor Frankl. After giving a cursory glimpse at the essence of logotherapy, and its emphasis on attitudes, meaning, will, and freedom, May goes on to state:

> But the dangers are that logotherapy hovers close to authoritarianism. There seem to be clear solutions to all problems, which belies the complexity of actual life. It seems that if the patient cannot find his goal, Frankl supplies him with one. This would seem to take over the patient's responsibility and—if we accept Rogers' assumption—diminish the patient as a person.[2]

Frankl himself is aware of this remark by May. He writes that

> logotherapy does not at all "hover close to authoritarianism," and least of all does it amount to "taking over the patient's responsibility and diminishing him as a person," . . . On the contrary, logotherapy can be defined as education to responsibility.[3]

Frankl obviously feels that May has missed the mark and misread logotherapy by even suggesting that logotherapy might impose solutions. May's comments, if valid, are serious charges which damage any claim logotherapy makes for clinical acceptability.

It seems vital, therefore, to analyze why May voices his skepticism and why Frankl rejects it as unfounded.

II

May and Frankl agree that psychotherapy is not value-free. In May's words, "values are presupposed at every point in the counseling process."[4] Frankl says that "there can be no medical practice untouched by values or ethical assumptions.[5] "Every school of psychotherapy has a concept of man, although this concept is not always held consciously."[6]

The philosophy of the therapist, conscious or unconscious, has great bearing on the direction therapy will take; whether it is toward release from tension or relief from an anxiety, or whether it is toward the fulfillment of the self or meaning in the world. For May, "our chief concern in therapy is with the potentiality of the human being. The goal of therapy is to help the patient actualize his potentialities."[7] Logotherapy, in Frankl's view, is geared to "helping others to see meaning in life."[8]

Is there any distinction between helping the patient "actualize his potentialities" and helping others "to see meaning in life"? In terms of end goals, May and Frankl probably are similar. They differ, however, on how best to achieve these goals. Superficially, the difference between the two is implicit in the titles of books they wrote. May's is titled *Man's Search for Himself*,[9] Frankl's is titled *Man's Search for Meaning*.[10] May and Frankl walk similar paths, but they part company at a precise fork in the road.

Philosophically, the world-views of May and Frankl orient around the notion of freedom. For Frankl, freedom is the first fundamental assumption of logotherapy.[11] In clinical terms, "the progress of therapy can be measured in terms of the progress of 'consciousness of freedom.'"[12] According to May, the patient at the beginning of therapy presents a picture of one who lacks freedom. The patient speaks of being driven, of being unable to know or choose, and thus unable to experience authentically. It is necessary to increase the patient's capacity to realize the extent to which he or she can be aware and can move in the world; or, in a word, to experience freedom.

Freedom, for May and Frankl, is not anarchy or arbitrariness. Freedom can never be separated from responsibility.[13] And, freedom "must be interpreted in terms of responsibleness."[14]

May and Frankl take almost identical approaches to the free will vs. determinism problem. For May

> the patient moves *toward* freedom and responsibility in his living as he becomes more conscious of the *deterministic* experiences in his life. . . . *Freedom* is thus not the opposite to determinism.[15]

Frankl sees deterministic forces not only as enlarging the scope of freedom, but as a basic requisite for free will.

> Freedom without destiny is impossible; freedom can only be freedom in the face of a destiny, a free stand toward destiny. Certainly man is free, but he is not floating freely in airless space. He is always surrounded by a host of restrictions. These restrictions, however, are the jumping-off points for his freedom. Freedom presupposes restrictions, is contingent upon restrictions.[16]

According to May, freedom *requires* the ability to accept, bear, and live with anxiety. To run away from normal anxiety is to surrender one's freedom. The flight from anxiety capitulates to the anxiety, and impedes the individual's ability to move in the world. Instead of the individual having the anxiety, the anxiety has the individual.

May's notion has its counterpart in the logotherapeutic view of suffering. In Frankl's words

> there is a suffering beyond all sickness, a fundamental human suffering which belongs to human life by the very nature and meaning of life.[17]

Frankl calls this type of suffering, which emanates from a frustration of man's quest for meaning, a human achievement, a "positive achievement in the highest sense of the term."[18]

The human being who has normal anxiety, who suffers the self into a better person, exhibits a truly human phenomenon. May and Frankl agree that administering drugs to alleviate this anxiety or suffering tranquilizes away the individual's capacity to grow.

May and Frankl perceive freedom as a potential to be actualized, rather than something which just is. Freedom is seen as a dynamic concept, as a "freedom toward" as opposed to the static concept of freedom as "freedom from." In the same sense, anxiety is viewed as "anxiety toward" rather than "anxiety from," suffering is "suffering toward" instead of "suffering from."

Though there are several obvious similarities, it should be clear that the concepts of freedom in May and Frankl are not identical.

For May, freedom seems to orient around the patient's confrontation with the self, around the concept of awareness in its distinctively human form, consciousness. May's system emphasizes the meaning of an individual's guilt for the individual.

> Our discussion of freedom indicates, however, that we should not as therapists and counselors transfer *our* guilt and *our* value judgments to the counselee and patient, but endeavor to help him bring out and confront *his* guilt and its implications and meaning for him.[19]

For Frankl, freedom links to the present and future. The patient is awakened to the freedom which inheres in everyone to take a stand toward instinct, heredity, environment, and suffering. The individual is shown the possibilities of transcending the present dilemma or predicament through taking a positive, optimistic, and in some cases humorous attitude to the situation or condition.

In other instances, the sense of frustration from lack of meaning, the emptiness which Frankl terms the "existential vacuum," is countered through encouraging the patient to focus on the meanings and values waiting to be actualized out there in the world. Logotherapy is a future-oriented philosophy which focuses on the value world and does not try to look into the past or dig into the self. The patient is linked with values rather than with the self.

III

May and Frankl walk similar paths, but they part company on the issue of self-fulfillment. May focuses on awareness, on consciousness, on the finding of one's self. May's ideal society is one which gives the maximum opportunity for each individual to realize the self.[20] His ethics are, in effect, an ethics of inwardness.

May asserts

> An ethical act, then, must be an action chosen and affirmed by the person doing it, an act which is an expression of his inward motives and attitudes. It is honest and genuine in that it would be affirmed in his dreams as well as his waking states. . . . one has endeavored to act as nearly as possible from the "center" of himself.[21]

In contrast, Frankl speaks of the objective world of meaning and values. Frankl rejects the valuation which is a

> mirroring of processes which go on in the individual in an impersonal way or merely as projections and expressions of the inner structure of the subject. . . . We have to take into account the objectivity of the world which alone presents a real challenge to the subject.[22]

According to Frankl, meaning is not invented, it is detected.[23] He states quite clearly that by "objective values" he means that these values "are necessarily more than a mere self-expression of the subject himself."[24] They stem, in Frankl's words, from a sphere beyond man and exist independent of the person. Philosophically, "objective values" seems to imply a revealed set of values, but Frankl uses the term "objective" to indicate that values *exist, unconditionally,* and that no person could ever be deprived of the possibility for actualizing values. The notion of "objective values," in the logotherapeutic view, is a clinical necessity.

For Frankl, cognition is founded on a polar tension between the objective value world and the subjective world of the person.[25] This dynamic process he calls "noodynamic."

In regard to the matter of self-actualization, Frankl claims:

> the true meaning of life is to be found in the world rather than within man or his own *psyche,* as though it were a closed system. By the same token, the real aim of human existence cannot be found in what is called self-actualization. Human existence is essentially self-transcendence rather than self-actualization. Self-actualization is not a possible aim at all, for the simple reason that the more a man would strive for it, the more he would miss it. For only to the extent to which man commits himself to the fulfillment of his life's meaning, to this extent he also actualizes himself. In other words, self-actualization cannot be attained if it is made an end in itself, but only as a side-effect of self-transcendence.[26]

Self-actualization is not negated by Frankl. He claims that the best way to achieve it is through orienting around the objective value world.[27] In practical terms, intending self-fulfillment is self-defeating.[28] The objective value world is the best means of achieving this fulfillment. One must be careful to actualize the values for their own sake, and not for the gain it may bring, for this reduces values to a tool and technique. Frankl thus radically rejects subjective self-expression.

The notion of an objective value world around which the person orients is a vital philosophical and clinical notion in logotherapy. Philosophically, there can be no situation in which the finite individual could complete the infinite, objective tasks of life.[29] The human being is in a perpetual process of becoming, by definition. If value-saturation were possible, it would suspend meaning and deny the person the opportunity for human achievement.

Clinically, this means there is no situation in life which must be relegated to meaninglessness. The possibility of realizing meaning is a basic fact of human existence. Even if creativity and the experience of life are closed off, the possibility of value realization remains.

> But even a man who finds himself in the greatest distress, in which neither activity nor creativity can bring values to life, nor experience give meaning to it—even such a man can still give his life a meaning by the way he faces his fate, his distress. By taking his unavoidable suffering upon himself he may yet realize values. Thus, life has a meaning to the last breath. For the possibility of realizing values by the very attitude with which we face our unchangeable suffering—this possibility exists to the very last moment.[30]

Values are objective and meaning is unconditional as well as realizable at all times. The logotherapist who treats someone suffering from existential despair will open up to the patient the infinite value world.

IV

The dispute between May and Frankl over the nature of logotherapy is rooted in their differences on the issue of self-expression versus self-transcendence and the ethics of inwardness versus the objective value world.

May's system focuses on self-perceived truth and the aware person searching consciously within the self, in freedom, to find these verities. From this perspective, it "seems" as if a world view which places values outside the person, in a trans-subjective or objective setting, is authoritarian.[31] In fact, it would be authoritarian if such a clinical approach *imposed* its philosophy on patients. Such a clinical relationship would rob the patient of individual freedom and "diminish the patient as a person." Choices would be made *for,* rather than *by* the patient.

May's is a therapy toward freedom and awareness. Frankl's is a therapy toward meaning. May suggests that logotherapy does in fact impose, or, in his words, "supply" the patient with meanings.

Frankl does not agree.

> The logotherapist does not "supply the patient with his goal." . . . If he ever did, he was not logotherapist.[32]

Frankl repeatedly insists that the logotherapist's task is to

> make the patient fully aware of his own responsibleness; therefore it must leave to him the option for what, to what or to whom he understands himself to be responsible. That is why a logotherapist is the least tempted of all psychotherapists to impose value judgments on the patient.[33]

It may be helpful, in trying to resolve the May-Frankl argument, to see how Frankl views the clinical situation theoretically and in practice. Obviously logotherapy is no panacea, as Frankl himself states explicitly. Generally, logotherapy is "open to cooperation with other approaches to psychotherapy."[34] It is directed particularly at those symptoms which can be directly linked to feelings of meaninglessness or dis-ease in the noological dimension.

As if he anticipates the type of criticism leveled by May, Frankl takes great pains to explain the dynamics of logotherapy.

> Existential analysis aims at nothing more and nothing less than leading men to consciousness of their responsibility. It endeavors to help people experience this element of responsibility in their existences. But to lead a person further than this point, at which he profoundly understands his existence as responsibility, is neither possible nor necessary.[35]

Insofar as responsibility itself is concerned, Frankl sees it as a formal ethical concept which does not contain any specific imperatives on conduct. It is ethically neutral in that it does not dictate toward what or whom the responsibility should be directed. Responsibility is an innate part of the human being. Logotherapy seeks to hone the sense of responsibility so that the person, in freedom, may make the meaning choices. This "precludes moralizing on the part of the therapist."[36]

Frankl contrasts the logotherapist with a painter, who paints the world subjectively. The logotherapist, rather, is like an ophthalmologist, who tries to enable the patient to see the world as it really is. "The logotherapist's role consists in widening and broadening the visual field of the patient so that the whole spectrum of meaning and values becomes conscious and visible to him."[37] The logotherapist tries to illuminate what is there, what is "objective" and real, and thus confront the patient with real choices.

The logotherapist attempts to show the patient that there is a meaning which is unique to each individual and which never ceases, up to and including the moment of death. The logotherapist hopes the patient will realize the unconditional meaninfulness of life and thus, through the search for meaning, transcend the immediate predicament.

However,

The logotherapist leaves it to the patient to decide what is meaningful and what is not, or, for that matter, what is good and what is bad.[38]

An excerpt from an actual case illustrates how logotherapy works in the clinical situation. The case concerns a nineteen-year-old art student who displayed severe symptoms of incipient schizophrenia. She considers herself as being confused and asks for help.

Patient: . . . What is going on within me?
Frankl: Don't brood over yourself. Don't inquire into the source of your trouble. Leave this to us doctors. We will steer and pilot you through the crisis. Well, isn't there a goal beckoning you—say, an artistic assignment?
Patient: But this inner turmoil. . . .
Frankl: Don't watch your inner turmoil, but turn your gaze to what is waiting for you. What counts is not what lurks in the depths, but what waits in the future, waits to be actualized by you. . . .
Patient: But what is the origin of my trouble?
Frankl: Don't focus on questions like this. Whatever the pathological process underlying your psychological affliction may be, we will cure you. Therefore, don't be concerned with the strange feelings haunting you. Ignore them until we make you get rid of them. Don't watch them. Don't fight them.
Imagine, there are about a dozen great things, works which wait to be created by Anna, and there is no one who could achieve and accomplish it but Anna. No one can replace her in this assignment. They will be your creations, and if you don't create them, they will remain uncreated forever. . . .
Patient: Doctor, I believe in what you say. It is a message which makes me happy.[39]

Within a few weeks the patient was free enough from her schizophrenic symptomatology that she was able to resume her work and study.

This example is particularly useful in that it offers a clear illustration of an approach which might be misconstrued as authoritarian. There is a thin but decisive line between opening up value potentials and imposing them. Logotherapy focuses, in the healing process, on the patient's future. It dereflects from the focus on the past and present, and tries to build on healthy future orientation. The clinical approach of logotherapy is toward confronting the patient with a future so that the patient may transcend the past. This future can be illuminated, but the values to be actualized in this future cannot be forced onto the patient. The approach differs from conventional psychotherapy, but is far removed from authoritarianism.

In the case cited here, Frankl concentrated on opening up the creative value world for the patient, to de-reflect her and channel her concern into a creative act. The value was presented, but *not imposed*. The patient was given something to ponder. Giving the patient a positive life view, even through convincing argument, is not the same as authoritarian coercion.

A key factor in this clinical situation is the personal charisma of Frankl himself.

> Any witness to Frankl's interview feels the impact of Frankl's personality, his genuine sincerity, his complete openness toward the patient, and his high respect for the other human being.[40]

V

In the closing page of his major work, Frankl takes a philosophical view of the reactions logotherapy can expect.

> The area we have entered with our logotherapy, and, above all, with existential analysis, is a borderland be-

tween medicine and philosophy. Medical ministry operates along a great divide—the dividing line between medicine and religion. Anyone who walks along the frontier between two countries must remember that he is under surveillance from two sides. Medical ministry must therefore expect wary glances; it must take them into the bargain.[41]

Criticisms of logotherapy such as May's require us to examine its philosophical and clinical position.

Logotherapy's philosophy is explicit and its clinical application is clear and precise. Thus, it compares favorably with other therapies in terms of the degree to which it enhances awareness, freedom, self-actualization, and the attainment of meaning.

RESPONSE TO BULKA'S PAPER
ROLLO MAY

In an issue of this sort it is best not to refer to one's writing about therapy (which can often be confusing) but to consider the actual encounters with patients. I submit that the case Bulka cites (on page 13) demonstrates very clearly what I have said about logotherapy "skating on the edge of authoritarianism."

In this therapeutic encounter there are three interchanges between the patient and Frankl. Frankl begins each one of them with a clear and unmistakeable "Don't." The first "don't" he emphasizes by adding another a little later in the sentence. Such categorical instruction illustrates the authoritarian character of logotherapy as practiced by Frankl to which I referred.

Frankl also promises the patient that the doctors, presumably representors of "this objective value system," will "take care of her." "We will cure you," he states. In my experience it is never constructive to take the person's initiative for cure entirely out of his or her own hands. To do this, I believe, also runs counter to the existential approach to human beings, which in my judgment rests upon the belief that however much the patient's sense of responsibility has been eroded, it needs to be built upon and enlarged. Frankl's patient ends up with a submissive statement, "I believe in what you say." This is almost the opposite to what I would hope a patient would say. It represents the removal of responsibility from the patient and puts it squarely on the shoulders of the doctor. The patient is asked to place unquestioning faith in the therapist. This has the same authoritarian character as fundamentalistic religion.

One might take the client's later apparent progress in handling her schizophrenic symptomatology as proof that this therapy worked. But schizophrenics in my experience are helped mostly by the nature of the relationship between the client and the doctor. Unfortunately, this relationship is not generally described. We are not given the opportunity to see the fuller context of the relationship between Frankl and this woman.

Logotherapy has made some important theoretical contributions to the overall theory of existential psychotherapy. But after reading this article I believe more clearly than ever that at times logotherapy "hovers on the edge of authoritarianism."

VIKTOR FRANKL

Bulka has included in his paper, as he has pointed out himself, only "an excerpt" from the dialogue I had with my patient Anna. He did not include, for example, my reference to the fact that what I had to deal with was an acute state of a somatogenic condition as evidenced, last but not least, by her "exhibiting the 'corrugator phenomenon,'" which I described in 1935 *(Zeitschrift fur die gesamte Neurologie und Psychiatrie* 152: 161). This condition "is characterized by fibrillar twitches of the corrugator muscles," and, as I could show at that time by autopsy findings, is symptomatic of a pathological process located in a certain area of the brain tissue.

The patient had been admitted to the Neuropsychiatric Department of the Poliklinik Hospital of Vienna and was shown to me by my staff in order to discuss the question of diagnosis and therapy. She not only was mentally disturbed and felt "confused," but also was hallucinating. Immediate therapeutic intervention was required, and in view of the obviously somatogenic origin of the psychological symptomatology, I ordered specific pharmacotherapy.

But I also wanted to say a few words to her, not as the Head of the Neuropsychiatric Department, but rather *as a human being to another human being.* As any other member of the medical profession would have done in such a case, I told her that the prognosis was good—a prediction that eventually proved correct. So I gave my patient (who understandably was in utmost despair) some hope—again something that any medical doctor would have felt compelled to do in my situation. But in addition to my efforts to enhance her hope for recovery and restore her capacity to work, I interspersed some remarks aimed at reducing her tendency to what is called "hyper-reflection" in logotherapy. In a case like that of Anna, hyper-reflection would have caused a psychogenic depression on top of the somatogenic condition. That is why I urged her "not to brood over herself, not to be concerned" with the hallucinations haunting her, "not to watch them, not to fight them."

Now, if anyone labels as authoritarian the fact that a medical doctor recommends to his patients to the best of his knowledge and for the sake of their recovery what they should do or should not do, I gladly take the blame. And if anyone labels it "authoritarian" if a medical doctor truthfully tells the patient that the prognosis is good, I gladly take the blame. But if the patient then says that she "believes" in the good prognosis and anyone compares this "faith" with "fundamentalistic religion," I as a member of a medical faculty must leave such a comparison to the judgment of members of theological faculties.

After thus having gladly taken several blames, there is something I do *not* take, and that is the credit for having cured Anna through logotherapy: she was cured through pharmacotherapy! And it was this treatment to which I had referred when telling her that she should "leave this to us doctors." Or should I have left it to her to invent and prescribe pharmacotherapy? Sorry, I was too "authoritarian" to leave this to her. Anyway, Bulka is to be congratulated, for his prophecy was fulfilled: in his paper he had spoken of the case of Anna as the "illustration of an approach which might be misconstrued as authoritarian." It then was, in fact, "misconstrued."

Chapter Two

PARADOXICAL INTENTION AND DE-REFLECTION: RETURN TO NATURALNESS

One of the truisms of straight thinking is that the surest way to achieve a goal is by willfully intending it and pursuing it. You don't get something for nothing. Success will not come to the individual as manna from heaven, it must be worked at and earned.

Besides the few who have made the jump from rags to riches, there are others who would gladly testify against this form of straight thinking. They include the enterprising entrepeneur whose expansion led to bankruptcy instead of wealth, the glory-seeker who was left with no friends and no meaning in life, the pleasure-seeker who found a few thrills but could not keep the process going and eventually found only frustration. These types will affirm that you cannot get what you want simply by wanting it.

These types as well as many people with phobias of differing intensity or other behavior problems can now be told something even more radical—that often, what people want is what they do not get. In order to get what you want, it is better sometimes to wish for the opposite.

Eddie Stinson found this out the hard way, and it saved his life. In 1916, he was caught in a tailspin. Once in such a spin, no flier had ever recovered. No matter how hard a pilot pulled back on the stick, the plane's nose would continue its twisting, uncontrollable descent. Stinson was aware of this and figured that he may as well die quickly and avoid the agony of trying to save himself. He pushed the stick forward for a steep dive. To his amazement, the spinning stopped and the plane recovered its normal course. The suicidal reaction was instead the saving one.

Motorists who are caught in a skid are constantly urged

to turn their wheels in the direction of the skid to regain control on an icy road. Straight thinking or naive instinct would suggest turning in the opposite direction, but straight thinking, as we are beginning to find out, is not always effective thinking. Sometimes, truth and functionality are perceived in paradox.

II

What is a paradox? It may be described as a proposition which is seemingly self-contradictory or absurd, but in reality expresses a possible truth. It is absurd to think that a suicidal reaction can be a saving one, or that going along with the direction of a skid instead of fighting it is the rescue mechanism. These are paradoxes, and they are by no means the only examples of paradoxical intention.

Paradoxical intention is a term coined by Viktor E. Frankl, the father of logotherapy, to describe an ingenious technique used by logotherapists and intuitive common-sense-oriented therapists in clinical and extra-clinical situations.

Logotherapy is generally referred to as the third Viennese school of psychotherapy, following the Freudian and Adlerian schools. Logotherapy is recognized as belonging, at once, to the humanistic and existential streams of psychology. It has developed specific clinical techniques, unlike other existential modes of psychotherapy. Paradoxical intention (PI) is one of them.

Let us now follow Frankl's own description which he gives in his paper titled "Paradoxical Intention and De-reflection,"[1] and enlarged upon in his book *The Unheard Cry for Meaning*.[2] A given symptom evokes a fearful expectation that the symptom might recur. Fear often carries with it a prophetic quality, in that the individual is likely to bring to realization the very object of fear. Anticipatory anxiety is likely to trigger precisely what the person fears. This sets off a vicious circle syndrome; the symptom evokes a phobia, the phobia induces the symptom, and the recurring symptom reinforces the phobia. A feedback mechanism is established and the patient is caught in a cocoon.

In cases of obsessive-compulsive neurosis, the patient fights against obsessions and compulsions, as opposed to phobias, which are characterized as flight from fear. In the case of the obsessive-compulsive, the fight strengthens the obsessions. Again, the patient is locked into a vicious circle of pressure inducing counterpressure, and counterpressure increasing the primary pressure.

It is the therapist's task to break the vicious circle. In PI, the phobic patient is encouraged to *do* that which is feared, and the obsessive compulsive is urged to *wish* the very thing which is feared.

The therapy is very clear and direct. A claustrophobic patient whose fear extended to flying, going in elevators, trains, buses, theaters, restaurants, any confined space, who feared, in fact, that she would choke or die, was told not to run away from the phobic situations. (There were precious few places left to run to, anyway.) Instead, she was to try to suffocate and die right on the spot, and to exaggerate her physical symptoms. Soon she was able to negotiate all these confined places, and to remain free of her previous symptoms.

The case of this patient was a phobia. The patient was urged to do that which was feared, to seek out the confining places, to meet the phobia head-on rather than fleeing from it.

In obsessive-compulsive situations, the patient is encouraged to wish what is feared. A patient with a washing compulsion so severe that it was necessary to start toileting at four in the morning in order to make a noon appointment was told and taught to wish that everything would be as dirty as possible. Gradually, the washing and dressing time was reduced until after a month's treatment in hospital the patient was able to resume regular professional duties. So far, Frankl's report.

III

PI can work instantly, but at times it takes more than a session or two to put the patient on the right track. Generally, acute cases of anxiety and obsessional neurosis respond within 4-12 sessions. Patients with disorders of several years duration will normally be cured within a year. Much depends, of course, on the therapist and the patient. There is, for instance, the story of a museum guard who could not remain on the job for fear that someone would steal a valuable painting. He was advised, "Tell yourself they stole a Rembrandt yesterday and today they will steal a Rembrandt and a Van Gogh." The guard exclaimed, "But that is against the law!" PI did not work in this instance, and there are other instances in which it does not work. In psychotherapy there are no panaceas and, as Frankl says, his logotherapy is no exception to this rule, but PI is very successful. A success rate of about 90% was reported by Dr. Hans O. Gerz, one of the foremost practitioners of PI as Clinical Director of the Connecticut Valley Hospital. Often it succeeds where long-term psychotherapy failed.

As with behavior therapy, skeptics conjectured that symptom substitution would occur with PI. In 1972 Solyom et al.[3] conducted experiments to investigate the efficacy of PI. They chose two symptoms of equal importance and frequency to the patients, and had the patient apply PI to one, leaving the other symptom as the control. In a relatively short time span (6 weeks), there was a 50% improvement in the target thoughts, and no new obsessive thought replaced the eliminated obsession. As Joseph Fabry, a leading thinker in logotherapy, once put it, using William Menninger's observation, it is not absolutely necessary to know the cause of the fire in order to extinguish it.

Recently, L. Michael Ascher[4] has come up with a controlled experimental validation of the clinical effectiveness of PI. Some of his findings are reported in the first issue of *The International Forum for Logotherapy*.[5]

PI is particularly useful as a self-help technique. Part of the reason why a therapist need not take so long when using PI is that once the patient picks up the knack, the rest is downhill. If often takes much encouragement and reassurance, but once the patient has amalgamated PI unto the self, it can be used by the patient almost independently.

For the general population, PI is a useful approach for a suddenly appearing symptom. Sometimes, PI is used without the user being aware it is PI. Sparky Anderson, the successful manager of the two-time World Champion Cincinnati Reds and their Big Red Machine, used PI prior to the fifth game of the exciting 1975 World Series with the Boston Red Sox. His target was Tony Perez, a major cog in the big red machine who had gone hitless in the four previous games. "Doggie," said Anderson to Perez, "do yourself a favor and don't get a hit for the rest of the World Series. You know those little boys of yours, Victor and Eduardo. If you don't get a hit, they can tell their kids someday grandpa set a World Series record that nobody else ever touched. Whatd'ya say?"

It is a matter of record that in the fifth game of the 1975 World Series, subsequent to Anderson's PI, Perez hit two home runs and batted in four runs, enabling Cincinnati to win, 6-2! But PI is still not a panacea.

PI is useful for everyday situations we sometime take as normal. A speaker about to address a gathering is nervous, legs fidgeting, mouth jittery. The natural inclination is to fight the nervousness. Next time you or a friend are confronted with such a situation, take the reverse approach. Say to yourself, and mean it—they have had speakers before, who have surely been nervous. But if they think they have seen nervousness, wait till they see me. I will knock my knees together so loudly the noise will be deafening. My mouth will be so jittery I will say at least 5 "uhs" for every intelligent word! The PI motto would be—*if you cannot beat the symptom, join it*.

It helps, of course, to have a sense of humor, to be able to laugh at yourself. People who take things too seriously and are too wrapped up within themselves are unlikely candidates for PI. Humor, according to Frankl's theory, is a manifestation of what he calls "self-detachment"—the individual's capacity to detach himself from his self, to look objectively at his self and joke about his own symptoms. Often the exercise of self-detachment will do just that to the symptom, detach it from the person.

IV

The next time you see an individual uptight before an exam or an experience, don't do the normal thing, which is to say "relax"; instead, urge on the nervousness, tell your friend to break the Guinness record for sweating, or break the world record for vibrations per minute! It might work. Telling the person to relax most often does not.

Hardly a person has not had a bout of hiccups, and it usually seems to come at the worst times. Instead of running away from it, try to purposely hiccup. You will probably fail, which means, paradoxically, that you have succeeded. Stuttering, too, yields to the machinations of PI.

Insomnia is a pervading malaise. The mistake people make when plagued with insomnia is that they try anything and everything to induce sleep, from pills to alcohol to more pills and more alcohol. It would be more helpful to save the body from drugs and the budget from unnecessary expenses. PI is cheap. Just make an insomniac resolve to stay awake, to do everything possible not to fall asleep. This must be done honestly, with both eyes open. Under normal circumstances, the sleep will ensue automatically.

PI defies generational boundaries. It is effective for elderly people who have gone through a major part of life with compulsions or phobias, and is also useful in treating children.

One teacher used PI for an 11-year-old who spent the

entire day in class staring at classmates. This aroused understandable resentment and led to a diminished self-image and loss of standing amongst peers for the child. Other techniques did not help, so the teacher tried PI. The student was told to stare at selected students for alternating periods of 15 minutes. The child's reaction pretty well describes any initial reaction to PI—". . . that sounds goofy." The young student tried it, and was amazed to find that suddenly staring had become impossible. Gradually, the child was weaned away from the staring, and gained a new stature with classmates and an improved self-image.

I tried PI myself a little while ago. We had suffered through the death of a 2-month-old son, who succumbed to SIDS (Sudden Infant Death Syndrome), commonly referred to as crib-death. My older children, 7 and 8 years old, were deeply affected by the tragedy. They would often break down in tears with no provocation. If I asked why they were crying they would say, "Daddy, you should know by now." This, after long and uninhibited discussions with them on the meaning of death and what had happened to their brother. The conversations would reassure them, but in their words, something would sometimes come into their throat, making crying uncontrollable. On one occasion, instead of asking them why they were crying, I told them to continue crying, but not about the past. I asked them to cry to God to send them another baby. They absorbed this, and, in a matter of seconds, had stopped crying. Not a miracle, simply PI at work.

It should be pointed out that PI success cannot be interpreted as merely a suggestive effect. Benedikt in 1968 subjected patients who had been treated successfully with PI to tests in order to evaluate their susceptibility to suggestion. The results showed they were even less susceptible than the average.

PI should not be administered for all symptoms. A person suffering from endogenous depression should not be encouraged, through PI, to commit suicide 15 times. Such a patient might actually try it only once.

And, the agoraphobic who fears the onset of a heart attack should not be encouraged to have a few heart attacks, and a stroke to boot, unless a cardiologist has checked the patient and found everything in order.

For the everyday symptoms, however, PI may be self-administered with confidence.

V

Logotherapy introduces another technique for situations which are not flight from fear, as in phobias, or fight against obsessions and compulsions, as in the obsessive-compulsive pattern, but are instead characterized by a fight *for* something, for sexual pleasure.

As Frankl points out again and again, the more the male tries to demonstrate his potency, the more he will fail; the more the female tries to show herself she is capable of orgasm, the more likely she is to become frigid. A vicious circle is here also likely to trap the pleasure-seekers. The patient pays excessive attention—or, as Frankl has called this, "hyper-reflection"—on the self to enhance performance and withdraws attention from the partner and the partner's arousal stimuli. Potency and orgasm are thusly diminished, enhancing the patient's "hyper-intention," to invoke another logotherapeutic term, and so on until impotence and frigidity occur.

As logotherapists have found, at least 90% of all sexual neuroses are rooted in the syndrome of hyper-intention and hyper-reflection.

For such cases of sexual dysfunction logotherapy uses the technique of de-reflection. The patient is de-reflected from striving for potency or orgasm and is instead reoriented toward the partner, forgetting the self and concentrating on the other. This approach is a specific application of the logotherapeutic view that, as Frankl puts it, "pleasure and happiness cannot be pursued but must ensue." Happiness, pleasure, even self-realization, are not achieved through intention but as a by-product, a side-effect of the fulfillment of meaning, or of loving another human being. The sex therapy used by logotherapy translates this meta-clinical philosophy into practical terms.

According to a technique that Frankl had developed—and published—as early as in the 1940's, the logotherapist tackles a potency problem by recommending to the patient that every sensual experience may be attempted, but that intercourse itself is strictly forbidden, for "medical" reasons. Such a pronouncement frees the patient from having to perform. If the patient returns after a week, and, as has occurred in many cases, apologetically tells the therapist that the advice was tried but intercourse came as a matter of course and could not be helped, the therapist, in mock anger, may further order the patient to desist for at least one more week. In one instance, the patient called back in midweek to say it was no use, they were having relations several times a day. The therapist's orders were not heeded, but the therapy itself succeeded. De-reflection as a technique is equally applicable in cases of frigidity. By not being concerned about orgasm, and instead concentrating on affectionately embracing the partner, orgasm is likely to ensue.

It is vital that the act of de-reflection be not merely a taking-the-mind-off the goal. There must be a positive redirection to something positive. In insomnia, for example, de-reflection is a useful technique. But it is futile just to tell the insomniac to take the mind off sleep. This works as well as motivated forgetting; it in fact ensures the perpetuity of the problem. The de-reflection from sleep must be directed toward something else, such as *counting sheep* or reading a book. In sexual dysfunction, the re-direction is toward dedication to the partner rather than concentration on sexual performance.

De-reflection, as PI, is a corrective where the natural flow has been impeded by unnatural reactions, such as "flight from, fight against, or fight for," to enumerate what Frankl calls the three principle patterns of neurotic reaction.

Naturalness and spontaneity are well illustrated in the story of a young boy who once approached Mozart and asked how to write a symphony. Mozart said, "You're a very young man. Why not begin with ballads?" The young boy protested, "You composed symphonies when you were 10 years old." "Yes," replied Mozart, "but I didn't ask 'how?'"

Life should not be manipulated through techniques, as an answer to the ubiquitous question "How?" Functionally it might work, but such an approach carries within it the seeds of disintegration.

Premature ejaculation is a prime manifestation of an unnatural approach to sex. It may lend itself to the PI treatment. A student of Frankl, for instance, told the patient not to worry about the premature ejaculation, as that would be unlikely to change anyway. He should therefore concentrate instead on reducing the duration of intercourse to one minute. In this case, the time needed to reach a climax was raised to five minutes by one week, and eleven minutes by the second week.

Logotherapy gains its greatest satisfaction not from being acclaimed as a new approach to therapy, but from the recognition that its approach is timeless, belonging in the sphere of common sense, or the wisdom of the ages. The fact that PI—a technique first written about by Frankl in 1939—has been compared to such relatively new techniques as flooding and implosion, or that de-reflection is a clear anticipation of the much publicized sex-therapy approach of Masters and Johnson indicates that therapy has taken a step back into the wisdom of the past. This step back has turned out to be a step forward. This in itself is paradoxical, but the many uses of paradox should have convinced the skeptic by now that there is indeed logic in paradox.

SECTION 2

LOGOTHERAPY AND RELIGION

PRELUDE

Logotherapy emphasizes the crucial factor of "meaning" in its motivational theory and at the same time has a positive attitude to genuine religiousness. It is, therefore, not surprising that it has attracted the interests of theologians from various denominations, some of whom even want to claim logotherapy on behalf of their particular faith systems. *Chapter Three* explores these claims and presents an analysis of the meaning of the multi-denominational pull.

Chapter Four is concerned with the question of whether logotherapy is, in fact, a spiritual therapy. Much of the material in this chapter is similar to the previous one, and even makes use of the conclusions reached in Chapter Three.

Logotherapy sees the term "spirit" in a non-parochialized way, much as it sees religion in a non-denominational way. The common thrust of this section shows how logotherapy accepts the particular but embraces the whole.

Chapter Three

THE ECUMENICAL INGREDIENT IN LOGOTHERAPY

It would seem an oddity, at best, to investigate the ecumenical ingredient in a psychological system. After all, the psychological dimension and the theological dimension are separated oft-times by an unbridgeable gap, and the most one is likely to expect from a disciplined psychological system is the faint hope of reconciliation with theological doctrine.

Such, however, is not the case with the logotherapeutic system of Dr. Viktor E. Frankl. Frankl's logotherapy is so imbued with concepts approximating a theological stance that many psychotherapists and theologians have read religious theory into logotherapy and logotherapy into religious theory. One must assuredly draw a line separating the speculative wishful thinking from the real fact. Nevertheless, it is an incontrovertible fact that logotherapy borders on theology,[1] and it would be instructive to discover the roots of its borderline theology and the possible implications for religion in general.

II

The fundamental thesis posited by logotherapy is that "the striving to find a meaning in one's life is the primary motivational force in man."[2] Humans are primarily spiritual beings, whose humanness is rooted in the spiritual dimension,[3] wherein is expressed the meaning potential indigenous to humans.

To be sure, Frankl does not deny the somatic and psychic elements in human beings, and the legitimate possibility that their behavior springs from these areas. Rather, Frankl posits the notion of our spirituality (spirituality taken not in its theological context but as the expression of what makes us human) as overarching the other dimensions, and potentially investing our instinctual aspects with spiritual motives. Spirit is then embracing of the whole rather than distinct from it.

The three basic assumptions upon which logotherapy is founded are (1) freedom of will, (2) will to meaning, and (3) meaning of life.[4]

Freedom of Will—Humans are always free to act according to their volition. It is acknowledged that certain factors in and around us are determining influences, but these determinants only prescribe boundaries, or what may be termed destiny. Within the circumscribed destiny that is shaped by instinct, heredity, and environment, we are forever free to take a stand for or against conditions, mainly through our attitude toward them.[5] Whether we use our cunning to become a thief or a lawyer, or our lust to spill blood to become a surgeon or a murderer, are attitudinal decisions which can be made in the freedom of our situation. "Man ultimately decides for himself!"[6]

Will to Meaning—We will to meaning rather than to pleasure or power. As deciding beings, we will our actions, rather than are driven by an inner force or urge. Existential persons are concerned with meanings as opposed to pleasure and power. Seeking pleasure as an ultimate goal is self-defeating, for the more one strives for pleasure, the more pleasure will elude one. The futility of this approach is most obvious in the sexual neuroses that develop out of one's focusing on the pleasure aspect of the sex act, instead of concentrating on the meaning aspect of fulfilling one's partner. As for power, experience shows that power is only a means for the more important task of meaningful accomplishment. Those who lust for power for powers' sake are usually denied it. The primary thrust of one's endeavor is towards finding a meaning in life, with pleasure a natural result of meaningful fulfillment, and power a means to meaning.[7]

Meaning of Life—There is an objective value world, a world filled with meaning. This meaning is beyond us in our subjective situation and exists outside and independent of us. This is the concept upon which is built the notion of the unconditional meaningfulness of life, in spite of all conditions and in all situations, including suffering and death. If meaning were subjective, it would be dependent on subjective judgment, thus possibly suspending the meaningfulness of a situation and destroying the unconditional meaningfulness of each moment. The meaning, as objective, is thus outside of us. To actualize meaning, we must reach beyond ourselves, transcend ourselves into the meaning dimension. Only when we focus beyond ourselves do we achieve the meaning which in the process provides automatic, albeit tangential, self-fulfillment.[8] There is thus a constant tension between the subjective "I am" and the object-ive "I ought," with the values of the cosmos eliciting from persons a transcending response urging a meaningful expression.[9]

To be sure, there are times when one might be frustrated by what one feels is the meaninglessness of one's situation. Frankl's notion of objective meaning merely asserts that "a" meaning is there to be detected. The conviction that every situation has its own unique meaning is the first premise of logotherapy, the underlining statement upon which logotherapy is built. Our inability to find the meaning does not negate the existence of a meaning, and part of the task of the logotherapist in a situation of existential despair is to help the patient discover meaning. Beyond this, having ostensibly discovered the meaning, one never really knows if the meaning one has discovered is the meaning that is meant. Frankl often quotes Allport's assertion that one can at the same time be half-sure and whole-hearted. One thus continually strives for an elusive, objective, quasi-mystical meaning, never knowing if one has reached it.

Frankl speaks of three types of values: (1) creative values, or what one gives to the world in terms of one's own positive contributions; (2) experiential values, or what one takes from life in terms of one's experience; and (3) attitudinal values, or the stand one takes toward an unchangeable aspect of one's existence.[10]

Frankl does not feel obliged to answer such questions as what is the source of the objective values. The theologian might be quick to jump on him and insist that this is a religious concept,[11] yet Frankl maintains that logotherapy is a secular system.[12]

Unconditional meaning, the natural emanation from the concept of objective values, is most questionable in the suffering situation, be it in the throes of agony over a tragic loss, or in the face of an inoperable cancer. While attempts are made to open up meaning possibilities which are beyond the suffering situation,[13] the ultimate resolution of the meaning of suffering belongs in the realm of the unknown.

Is it not possible that there is still another dimension possible, a world beyond the human world; a world in which the question of an ultimate meaning of human suffering would find an answer?[14]

Here again logotherapy invites the theologian to ask whether this is not really afterlife in humanistic terminology.

Logotherapy turns around the standard "what can I expect of life?" question by claiming that really life confronts one,[15] and one is asked to respond to the demands of life. In this response-iveness one actualizes one's responsibility. The objective value situation, what is called life, might be called "God" by the religious person.

At this point, it is unnecessary to delve further into the basics of logotherapy, not because such a probe would not yield significant results, but because most of logotherapy is rooted in the fundamental notions herein outlined. For the purposes of this article, the next step is to present the reactions of students of logotherapy relative to the religious aspect.

III

It is noteworthy to point out that Frankl himself is singularly aware of the hazards of his position. While being admittedly a man of faith,[16] Frankl refuses to let that faith spill over into logotherapy.[17] Frankl even acknowledges that his system ultimately leads to faith. In the final analysis it must certainly appear questionable whether humans could really be responsible before something—or whether responsibility is only possible when it is before someone.[18] A more assertive statement is that "the true discovery of man, the *inventio hominis,* occurs in the *imitatio Dei.*"[19] Beyond this, Frankl even shows some clinical implications for the condition which he calls repressed religiousness.[20]

Still in all, logotherapy, which is geared to the spiritual person, is seen as secular. Frankl even goes to great pains to assure his readers that when he uses "spiritual" to describe persons, it is divorced from any religious connotation[21] and means merely the dimension of specifically human phenomena. Logotherapy, it is true, is open to the religious person, but at the same time it is also open to the atheist and agnostic.[22] Frankl insists on respecting the authenticity of religious expression,[23] and indeed this is a noteworthy development in the field of existential psychology, but he fiercely resists the temptation and pressure to advocate, in logotherapy, a religious stance.

In general, most critics of logotherapy are aware of its relation to theology. Ungersma,[24] Tweedie,[25] Patterson,[26] and others appreciate Frankl's intent in separating religion from logotherapy, though there is great doubt whether he has succeeded in this task. It is one thing to caution the clinician not to impose any religious doctrine on the patient,[27] but it is quite another to separate the theology from the theory when that theology is so manifest. Birnbaum calls the aspect of meaning para-religious,[28] but others are not that restrained.

> If values are not only objective but absolute, as Frankl further contends, they must be given to us, discovered by us, but cannot have their origin in us. In that case, the question is legitimate: What has created them?[29]

These authors further attack the notion of one's responsibility to life.

> If "golden bridges" are to be built let them go from solid ground to solid ground; from the human creature dependent upon God his maker and responsible to Him for every thought, word, and deed, to the need of the present moment and the opportunity it provides for living one's life. They are not to be raised on the neutral ground of a vague responsibility to a nebulous life of which full many a man these days has said: *Je m'en Fiche!*[30]

So much for the internal approach, which attempts to explore the intrinsic essence of logotherapy and its relation to religion.

There is no shortage of scholars who attempt to extend the principles of logotherapy into specific religious domains. Tweedie sees an affinity between logotherapeutic anthropology and a Christian view of persons.[31] He compares the idea of trichotomy and the logotherapeutic emphasis on the spiritual dimension.[32] He asserts that the logotherapeutic concept of the spirit closely approximates the biblical concept of the heart.[33] He parallels the notion of transcendence with one's relation to one's Creator.[34] Of course, these are areas of common ground, and, while they might facilitate the religious psychotherapist, they do not necessarily impute religion to logotherapy.

Leslie has compiled a collection of illustrative examples of logotherapy in New Testament incidents.[35] He sees room for comparing the notions of responsibility, values, will to meaning, and the meaning of suffering with Christian thought.[36] Others such as Fox[37] and Ungersma[38] also develop their theme along these lines.

At the same time, a number of scholars have attempted to show the relatedness of logotherapy to Judaism. It is pointed out that Frankl is a Jew; and thus there are unconscious elements that should be accounted for in his theory.[39] Frankl himself makes frequent use of Talmudic quotations, though the quotes are used in a supportive capacity.[40]

Leo Baeck saw logotherapy as *the* Jewish psychotherapy.[41]

One might take this as meaning the psychotherapy most readily adaptable to Judaism. Attention is given also by Amsel,[42] Grossman,[43] and Salit[44] to the common ground of logotherapy and Judaism in such areas as values and meaning, free will, self-transcendence, pleasure-seeking, suffering, repentance, and affirmation of life.

More recently this author has presented a preliminary study of the philosophical comparisons between logotherapy and Judaism.[45]

With logotherapy avowing a secular stance, and with the pulls exerted upon it by those who see theology in it, as well as by those who see more specific religious connotations in it, there appears to be an essential dilemma in coming to grips with what logotherapy is all about.

IV

The perplexities surrounding logotherapy, what it is and what it ought to be, cannot really be understood unless one understands the man behind the theory, Frankl himself.

There is a spirit to the man which is implicit throughout his works, a spirit which is explicit in his everyday life, that breathes an indomitable love for humanity. Only Frankl, a survivor of the concentration camps, could still assert that he favored a world in which Hitler were possible to a world in which we were controlled, with no choice for good or evil and thus with no meaning. Frankl's is an embracing love of humankind, and it would be unthinkable for him to deny himself or his logotherapy to any human person because of faith or lack of it. It is this spirit which works in Frankl, to the point that he creates great philosophical problems in his theory. He acknowledges the difficulties,[46] but refuses to take any stand which would restrict logotherapy to any faith. Only in this light can the secular nature of logotherapy be understood.

In a way, Frankl is happy that Judaism and Christianity are pulling logotherapy into their theologies, for the pull of the one negates the other, leaving logotherapy neutral.[47] Thus, in the development of logotherapy, Viktor Frankl has opened the psychiatrist's door not to any one particular religion, but to religion itself.[48]

The door is open, but the decision as to whether to pass the door or not is entirely the patient's.[49]

Frankl realizes that the notion of unconditional meaning in logotherapy comes so close to theology, most specifically when wrestling with the question of ultimate meaning. Given the crucial position of this concept within the logotherapeutic framework, it becomes imperative to translate this concept into acceptable secular terms. For one who cannot subscribe to Providence, Frankl offers the following explication:

> We can therefore at best grasp the meaning of the universe in the form of a super-meaning, using the word to convey the idea that the meaning of the whole is no longer comprehensible and goes beyond the comprehensible.[50]

Ultimate meaning is thus ultimate incomprehensibility, or supermeaning. "The more comprehensive the meaning, the less comprehensible it is."[51]

Upon close reflection, it turns out that the notion of incomprehensibility has definite theological implications for Frankl. He is impressed with the reference to God as "the Great Secret."[52] He asserts that "one cannot speak *of* God but only *to* God."[53] This is what is meant by prayer.[54] With regard to the question of whether God is dead, Frankl expounds:

> I would say that God is not dead but silent. Silent, however, he has been all along. The "living" God has been a "hidden" God all along. You must not expect him to answer your call. If you probe the depth of the sea, you send off sound waves and wait for the echo from the bottom of the sea. If God exists, however, he is infinite, and you wait for an echo in vain. The fact that no answer comes back to you is proof that your call reached the addressee, the infinite.[55]

Thus, for Frankl, "religion is man's awareness of the super-human dimension, and the basic trust in ultimate meaning residing in that dimension."[56] "He is the unknown God, and theology is the equation of the unseen."[57]

Frankl sees faith as a matter of trust in the ultimate meaning of life. But trust implies lack of knowledge, for there would be no need for trust if we knew. Precisely because we do not, indeed cannot, know the meaning—as it is a super-meaning, an incomprehensible—precisely for this reason is faith as trust in ultimate meaning a necessity.[58] Faith thus becomes the acceptance of the incomprehensibility of the whole. For Frankl, this is a more profound form of religiousness than trying to probe into, and rationalize, God's actions.[59] The super-meaning idea which Frankl appropriates to logotherapy is thus seen to approximate the essential religious views of Frankl.

This theology of the unknown and the unknowable as a basic corollary of the notion of unconditional meaning is for Frankl an all-inclusive one that can even be espoused by the so-called non-religious. Frankl subscribes to Einstein's idea that finding an answer to the question "What is the meaning of life?" is to be religious.[60] With this view it is easy to fit humanity into the category of religious.

What, then, of atheism? The answer, as might be expected, is that the atheist, too, possesses religious underpinnings. "The pathos of atheism is based on an implicit religious ethos; and the passion of the unreligious includes a hidden love of God."[61]

What, then, of the avowed secularity of logotherapy? The unavoidable response is that logotherapy must be secular, for only then could it be available to everyone, religious and secular. It is a secular discipline open to the religious dimension. The reader as well as previously cited authors might be convinced of the religiosity of logotherapy, and might question, on philosophical grounds, its ability to be at once secular and open to religion. To understand this anomaly on philosophical grounds might tax the intellect beyond measure. The point to keep in mind at all times is that logotherapy stems from an all-embracing ecumenical ethos on the part of Frankl, who will not, even in the face of possible contradiction, deny logotherapy to anyone. For the non-religious, it is the unknown and unknowable. For the religious, each faith can fill in the unknown with its own peculiar system of myths and symbols.[62] The non-religious admit the unknowability without attempting religious expression as a way of approaching the unknown, and it is left to each religious system to fill in the specific approaches to the riddles of life.[63]

As much as Frankl is pressed to espouse a theological stance, he nevertheless fiercely continues to resist it. In my own wrestlings with him,[64] he repeatedly said that he appreciated the grievances, but insisted that any step into theology must be left to the rabbi, priest, or minister. Frankl is willing to take the philosophical risks, as long as his logotherapy, which is, in a very definite way, *a religion for the non-religious,* remains open to all. Any serious student of logotherapy must take into account this ecumenical spirit in tackling the viability of logotherapy.

It is the self-negating aspect of logotherapy which is so overwhelming, and the live personality of Frankl which is so evident, in the formulation of the theory. One might say, in logotherapeutic terms, that Frankl has transcended the dictates of science and, in the process, has afforded all persons the real possibility of meaningful fulfillment. Logotherapy, in the clinic and in meta-clinical situations, is a most unique and authentic vehicle for universal "monanthropism."[65]

Chapter Four

IS LOGOTHERAPY A SPIRITUAL THERAPY?

Logotherapy is the unique contribution of Viktor E. Frankl to thought and the world of the clinic. It has been referred to as the third Viennese school of psychotherapy and is presently making a definite impact in many aspects of human life.

Logotherapy has been described as "healing through meaning." The term "healing" implies something medical whilst "meaning" implies a philosophy. In fact, logotherapy is an interesting mix of medicine and philosophy. It is at once a philosophy of human existence and a psychological theory based on this philosophy.

Frankl claims that "every school of psychology has a concept of man, although this concept is not always held consciously."[1] The concept of man proposed by logotherapy is translated directly into the clinical and metaclinical situation, so that any understanding of the dynamics of logotherapy must be founded on a full appreciation of its philosophy. Furthermore, as Allport notes, philosophy dare not be divorced from the clinical situation, as often philosophy itself is a clinical tool.

> May not (sometimes at least) an acquired world-outlook constitute the central motive of a life and, if it is disordered, the ultimate therapeutic problem?[2]

Logotherapy is rooted in the existential tradition and emphasizes the empirical wisdom of the "man in the street." For example, it illustrates the validity of the importance of meaning through reference to a study conducted by Johns Hopkins University and sponsored by the National Institute of Mental Health. This study showed that of 7,948 students at forty-eight colleges, 78% gave as their first goal "finding a purpose and meaning to my life."[3]

The existential vacuum born of frustration from lack of meaning in life was found in 80% of Viennese younsters from a sample of 500, and 60% of Frankl's American students.[4] Admittedly, it is a bit dangerous to use the wisdom of the "man in the street" as validation of any principle, as philosophy cannot and should not be based on opinion polls. However, these studies do at least indicate that the yearning for meaning is not a preposterous proposition and indeed must be taken seriously by any well-meaning clinician or philosopher.

Empirical evidence is useful in detecting problems. Philosophical wisdom buffered by clinical validation is a balanced approach to the solution. Frankl admits that

> in spite of our belief in the potential humanness of man we must not close our eyes to the fact that humane humans are, and probably will always remain, a minority.[5]

In true Franklian fashion, he then asserts that for this reason we are all challenged to join the minority, to become humane humans. Logotherapy is primarily concerned with eliciting from the individual ultimate human potential, as it views the exercise of this humanness as the essential condition of health.

II

In coming to grips with the question "Is Logotherapy a Spiritual Therapy?" it is vital to look upon the term "spiritual" in two contexts. There is the context which is used by Frankl and the context which one normally associates with the term "spiritual." The term "spiritual" is normally associated with the religious dimension, the dimension of faith. Frankl asserts that humans are primarily spiritual beings whose humanness is rooted in the spiritual dimension, wherein the meaning potential unique to humans is expressed. Frankl does not deny the existence of the somatic and psychic elements in human beings and the realistic possibility that behavior often springs from these areas. However, Frankl proposes the notion of the spiritual as overarching the somatic and psychic dimensions and potentially investing even instinctual aspects of human behavior with spiritual motives. Spirit is embracing of the whole rather than distinct from it.

Frankl's context of the term "spiritual" is not the equivalent of the religious dimension. He takes great pains to explain that the term "spiritual," as he uses it, is divorced from any religious connotation[6] and means merely the dimension of specifically human phenomena.

The misunderstanding concerning the term spiritual, as Frankl uses it, is rooted in a translation problem. In the original German, he uses the word "geistig," which means spiritual in the human sense, whilst "geistlich" means spiritual in the religious sense. The translators of Frankl's works used the term spiritual loosely, thus distorting the precise meaning as it is evident from the German. Frankl, in his own English writings, carefully avoids this misuse by using the terms "noological" and "noetic," to differentiate from the psychological and psychic, respectively, and to distinguish from the spiritual dimension in its religious sense.

It would be useful to explore the spiritual (distinctly human dimension) as conceived by logotherapy as the first step towards understanding how logotherapy relates to the spiritual dimension in its religious context.

According to logotherapy "the striving to find a meaning in one's life is the primary motivational force in man."[7] The essential philosophical notions surrounding the human dynamic are (1) freedom of the will; (2) the will to meaning; and (3) the meaning of life.[8]

III

The notion of *freedom of the will* asserts that the human being is free to search for and find meaning, at all times and in all circumstances. Instinct, heredity, and environment are factors which shape human destiny, but do not dictate it. "The person has instincts but instincts do not have the person." They are part of the shaping process, the restrictions within which human choice is reasonable and possible.

Frankl argues quite forcefully that freedom without destiny is impossible;

> freedom can only be freedom in the face of a destiny, a free stand toward destiny. Certainly man is free, but he is not floating freely in airless space. He is always surrounded by a host of restrictions. These restrictions, however, are the jumping-off points for his freedom. Freedom presupposes restrictions, is contingent upon restrictions.[9]

Logotherapy here very subtly introduces a dialectic approach in which the problem itself is seen as the solution. It all depends on the human attitude to specific situations. Even regarding restrictions the person remains free to decide what attitude to take to these restrictions. In "self-detachment" one is able to accept or reject. The spiritual aspect of attitude, or human choice, is the key factor. Free will, to be sure, is, in Frankl's view, merely a potential. Human beings who do not exercise free will indeed do not have it, but the potential to use it is always there. "Freedom is not freedom from conditions," says Frankl, "instead, it is freedom to take a stand toward whatever conditions may confront us."

IV

This leads to the second essential notion, the *will to meaning,* which may be seen as the mediating principle between the human being, the "subject," and the world of values, the "object." The individual who is free and exercises humanness *wills* toward meaning. The human being is not driven toward meaning, else this entire process would be devoid of choice and lacking true spiritual content. The will to meaning is a spiritual act, again spiritual in Frankl's sense of the term. Pleasure, Frankl claims, is not the prime goal of the human being because as such it is self-defeating and elusive. He illustrates this with the correlation between sexual neuroses, even impotence, and the "hyper-intention" on the pleasure in sex instead of the human aspect of fulfilling the other.

Clinically, logotherapy would suggest an approach which dereflects from pleasure and orients toward "dedication to a cause greater than oneself or to a person other than oneself," as Frankl recently put it in a lecture. It is immediately apparent that logotherapy does not moralize. There seems to be a two-way-street between the world of philosophy and the world of the clinic, in which clinical experience gives birth to a philosophical notion which is reinforced by its clinical efficacy. The concept of pleasure is a prime example of how logotherapy relates the spheres of philosophy and psychology.

Power, as Frankl asserts, is not an end in itself, it is rather a means for fulfillment, again validated by the self-defeating nature of the power which is sought. Even self-realization is not an end in itself; it is rather a side effect of "self-transcendence," to introduce this logotherapeutic concept. In striving for values and meaning, the actualization comes on its own, as a tangential side-effect. In other words, in Frankl's own words, "like pleasure, also 'self-realization' cannot be pursued, it must ensue."

The frustration of the will to meaning leads to what Frankl calls "existential frustration," and having no meaning leads to the *"existential vacuum"* and the development of *"noogenic neuroses."* The emptiness that becomes readily apparent the first Sunday after the football season is over or in situations of unemployment are prime examples of this neurosis. Indeed, there exist "Sunday neuroses" and "unemployment neuroses." Added to this, James C. Crumbaugh's Purpose-in-Life test which measures individual sense of purpose shows a definite relationship between low P-I-L scores and drug involvement, alcoholism, and criminality.[10] Lacking meaning and purpose, one is likely to seek artificial or aberrant thrills.

V

If the individual wills towards meaning, then there must be a *meaning of life,* which is the third essential notion in logotherapy. There is, according to logotherapy, an uncondiotional meaningfulness of life in any and all circumstances. Meaning is realized through values and it bridges the gap between the subjective "I am" and objective "I ought." In freedom, the human being chooses and wills to actualize the objective meaning. By objective is meant the proposition that meaning is not human invention, but a matter of discovery, or, as Frankl is used to saying, "meaning cannot be given, but must be found, and it has to be found by oneself."

According to logotherapeutic teachings, there are *creative* values, or "what one gives to the world," *experiental* values, or "what one takes from the world" in terms of experience, and *attitudinal* values, or "the attitude one takes" to a specific predicament or unchangeable fate. Value realization can never be suspended, else the essential dynamics which are necessary for human beings to exercise their humanness would, at some point in time, be cut off from human experience. The values therefore cannot be subjective, rather they must be objective and independent of any subjective state.

Values and meaning are often used interchangeably. Values are "meaning universals"; that is to say, "the unique meaning of today is the universal value of tomorrow."[11] If values are out there in the world, then it is the obligation of the individual to respond to the demand implied in the existence of value. In the spiritual condition of the individual, it is life which confronts and demands value realization. One is not to ask what life can give, instead one is obliged to ask what can be given to life.

> Ultimately, man should not ask what the meaning of his life is, but rather he must recognize that it is he who is asked. In a word, each man is questioned by life; and he can only answer to life by *answering for* his own life. To life he can only respond by being responsible.[12]

Again, this is a philosophical notion validated by the clinical and meta-clinical evidence which indicates that those who commit themselves to life, do not ask life to give them anything in particular and instead give to life meaning and value, find that life relates positively to them and brings them the benefits of fulfillment.

The human approach is extended to various life situations, with special emphasis on suffering, death, love, and work.

VI

There are several types of suffering. In physical suffering or the pains prior to death, the attitude is the key. Logotherapy tries to elicit meaning even from the suffering situation. By giving suffering a meaning, one can bear it and perhaps even overcome it. Frankl's own concentration camp experiences indicated that those who had a meaning in the suffering, perhaps a future point around which to orient, were better candidates for survival.

Where the suffering is the pain prior to death, it is much more difficult to suggest a future orientation. One might here open up the possibilities of a superworld, a world beyond the human dimension in which the meaning of suffering might be explicated. Such a proposition might be opened up as a possibility but not forced down the patient's throat. A logotherapist will certainly avoid any imposition of his own world view or value system on the patient.

There is a third type of suffering,

> a suffering beyond all sickness, a fundamental human suffering which belongs to human life by the very nature and meaning of life.[13]

This is existential suffering. The existence of this type of suffering in the individual is seen as a healthy sign and it is the first step towards confrontation with the world of values. As Frankl once so aptly said, when addressing the prisoners at San Quentin prison, "Due to his freedom of choice, man has the privilege to become guilty; but he also has the responsibility to overcome his guilt—to rise above himself—to grow beyond himself." In taking a proper attitude toward one's past, the future possibilities become realizable. All depends on the key spiritual aspect of attitude.

VII

In death, the human being *is*. Rilke once wished that all people be allowed to die their own death. Death is seen as the final imprint on life. Death in itself is incomprehensible. Our view is a this-worldly view, but Frankl suggests that death might not be a going to sleep, it might instead be a "being wakened." A healthy attitude to death is vital. Studies have shown that fear of death is often linked to a low P-I-L score.[14] This would indicate that those who fear death have not approached life properly, i.e., as an opportunity to fulfill meaning. In being confronted with death, one becomes aware that postponement is a waste of precious and irretrievable time.

Death introduces the notion of human finiteness in quantity and quality. There is the death of the human being in time, which may be called "temporality," and the death of time in the human being, which may be termed "singularity." Man's existence is a responsibility springing from man's finiteness. Responsibility itself must be understood in terms of temporality and singularity.[15] Life is irrepeatable. Every moment is either forever lost or forever preserved. Frankl therefore proposes as a categorical imperative, "live as if you were living for the second time and had acted as wrongly the first time as you are about to act now."[16]

Suffering guards from psychic rigor mortis, says Frankl.

We may add: death guards against procrastination. There is no room for perfection as a reality. It is something to strive for, but human finiteness and mortality make this an elusive and necessarily unachievable goal. Perfection would destroy the continual striving process and create a situation where values could not be realized. Perfection, therefore, is an undesirable human state.

Imperfection makes for uniqueness. If all individuals were perfect, says Frankl, they would all be the same, easily replaceable and interchangeable. The attitude logotherapy takes to its philosophy is consistent with the attitude it recommends in the clinic; namely, to see the reality of life in its positive context, in the light of potential meaning.

In death, a human being *is,* and what has been achieved always remains; "having been is also a kind of being—perhaps the surest kind."[17] As Frankl would say, "man's own past is his true future."[18] This obviously goes against the flow of a society which admires youth and its unlimited potential. Logotherapy questions whether future potentialities are better than past realities. This philosophical approach has obvious benefits in any therapeutic situation involving the aged or the dying.

Life is what one gives to it, and is a quality rather than a quantity. There is more meaningfulness in a short life properly lived than in a long and extended life which is meaningless. All evolves around the human contribution.

VIII

Love is a spiritual union. In Frankl's view, it is the experience of another individual in all that individual's uniqueness and singularity. Love is based on what Frankl calls self-transcendence; that is, the individual's being immersed in the other. However, love is not merely an I-thou situation. In the beauty of I-thou, the partners transcend towards the objective value world. Where love is expressed as a truly human phenomenon, fidelity is automatic. One loves not what the other "has," but what the other "is." Sex, therefore, is not that which leads to love; according to Frankl, sex is rather the bodily expression of something meta-sexual, namely, "love."

Frankl conceives of life as a task to which the human being must respond. With regard to the work situation, he insists that "the job at which one works is not what counts, but rather the manner in which one does the work."[19] It is the human ingredient with which the work is invested which is the key factor. The status of the individual is less vital than the unique contribution of the individual. The gas station attendant who responds to the call in full humanness is to be more admired than the callous doctor.

Even outside the work scene, it is possible to find meaning in life. There is a false identification of one's calling with the life task to which one is called. The life task to which one is called may find its expression even in situations of unemployment. Understandably, the first advice a logotherapist would give to the unemployed would be to earnestly seek a job. However, in the temporary unavailability of a job, logotherapy attemps to remove the despair of joblessness by opening the individual to the human tasks which are readily available for fulfillment, even without prospect of material gain.

IX

A key technique introduced by Frankl as early as in 1939 is paradoxical intention, which also emanates from the "self-detachment" capacity of the human being. Paradoxical intention may be used to correct anything from hiccups to insomnia. It concerns itself with the obsessive compulsive patient, who figths against obsessions and compulsions, and the phobic patient, who flees from fear. In paradoxical intention, the phobic patient is encouraged to *do* that which is feared, and the obsessive compulsive is urged to *wish* the very thing which is feared. A claustrophobic patient who fears flying, elevators, trains, and buses, and fears choking might result, is told to try to suffocate and die right on the spot. The obsessive compulsive with a washing compulsion is taught to wish that everything be as dirty as possible. The human ability to laugh at one's predicament is mobilized in paradoxical intention.

The other logotherapeutic technique, "dereflection," is used, as has been previously mentioned, in cases of sexual neurosis. The insomniac, too, can use dereflection, by reflecting away from sleep toward another activity such as counting sheep or reading a book. Human choice, attitude, and control are key elements in this approach.

X

This cursory presentation of logotherapy shows how it fuses together philosophical notions with clinical wisdom, with both philosophy and psychology feeding into each other. Logotherapy, at all times, focuses its concern on the distinctly human aspects of life and, in situations where problems arise, seeks to mobilize the human potential to effect a positive reorientation. Within the context of Frankl's equating the distinctly human with the term "spiritual," logotherapy presents itself as a spiritual therapy.

Precisely because many of the logotherapeutic concepts border on theology, it is important to understand logotherapy's relation to the spiritual world of religion. Frankl views religion as a human phenomenon which must be viewed positively in the clinical situation.[20] However, one understates the religious aspect relative to logotherapy merely by saying that logotherapy is open to religion, which indeed it is, as it is also open to the atheist and agnostic.[21]

Existence, in Frankl's view, is seen as rooted in the unconscious. "The foundation of existence is never and cannot be fully reflected upon and thus cannot be fully aware of itself."[22] "In its very origin, the human spirit is unconscious spirit."[23]

Conscience itself is the voice of transcendence and "an irreligious man is one who does not recognize this transcendent quality."[24] It is against this background that Frankl is able to say that "the pathos of atheism is based on an implicit religious ethos; and the passion of the unreligious includes a hidden love of God."[25]

Even though Frankl is convinced of the value of religion, it is not the clinical obligation of the logotherapist to push religion onto the patient since "to genuine religiousness man cannot be driven by an instinct—nor pushed by a psychiatrist."[26]

Frankl is admittedly a man of faith,[27] but he refuses to let that faith spill over into logotherapy.[28] There are those who claim that Frankl has not really kept religion out of logotherapy. Birnbaum calls the aspect of meaning para-religious.[29] Arnold and Gasson are less restrained. For them,

> If values are not only objective but absolute, as Frankl further contends, they must be given to us, discovered by us, but cannot have their origin in us. In that case, the question is legitimate: What has created them?[30]

Frankl himself, in coming to grips with the problem of the meaning of the whole, suggests the following explication.

> We can therefore at best grasp the meaning of the universe in the form of a super-meaning, using the word to convey the idea that the meaning of the whole is no longer comprehensible and goes beyond the comprehensible.[31]

Ultimate meaning is, in essence, ultimate incomprehensibility, or super-meaning. "The more comprehensive the meaning is, the less comprehensible it is," says Frankl. This notion of incomprehensibility has definite theological implications. Frankl is impressed with Leo Baeck's reference to God as *the great secret*.[32] "He is the unknown God, and theology is the equation of the unseen."[33]

Frankl views faith as a matter of trust in the ultimate

meaning, but trust implies absence of certainty, for there would be no need for trust if we knew. Since we do not and cannot know the meaning as it is a super-meaning, an incomprehensible, precisely for this reason is faith expressed as trust in ultimate meaning a necessity, an acceptance of the incomprehensibility of the whole. Frankl sees this as a more profound form of religiousness than attempting to probe into and rationalize God's actions.[34]

The super-meaning idea which Frankl proposes in his logotherapy seems to approximate his own religious views. Frankl directs logotherapy toward the ultimate unknown, but his approach is patterned in such a way that the atheist as well as the religious of each denomination can fill in the unknown with their own particular systems of myths and symbols.[35]

> The non-religious admit the unknowability without attempting religious expression as a way of approaching the unknown, and it is left to each religious system to fill in the specific approaches to the riddles of life.[36]

Frankl does question whether humans can really be responsible before something or whether responsibility is only possible when it is before someone. He asserts that "the true discovery of man, the *inventio hominis,* occurs in the *imitatio Dei.*"[37]

It seems that the philosophy of logotherapy is a bit more than merely a borderline theology. I have referred to it, in fact, as a "religion for the non-religious."[38] Frankl addresses himself to the human dilemma by undressing the denominational particularism of institutionalized religions and formulating an approach to life which is open to everyone. Frankl is aware of the religious element in logotherapy but refuses to parochialize it. He insists rather on maintaining logotherapy's availability to all individuals. For Frankl, the spiritual dimension in the human being is embracing of the whole. The spiritual dimension of life must, therefore, be embracing of all humankind. The essence of logotherapy is thus a unique therapy of and for the spirit.

SECTION 3

LOGOTHERAPY AND JUDAISM

PRELUDE

Ironically, the faith system with which logotherapy is most akin—Judaism—has been the least cognizant of this affinity. This author has endeavored to show how logotherapy and Judaism parallel each other in so many ways. *Chapter Five* offers some personal glimpses of Frankl from this writer's relationship with him, and develops, in a general way, the relevance of Frankl's thought for Jewish thinkers.

Chapter Six, in a more precise way, compares many of logotherapy's basic principles with Talmudic counterparts. The similarities are intriguing, as are the implications of these similarities.

Finally, a more in-depth view of the philosophy underlining logotherapy and how it compares with Judaic philosophy is the subject of *Chapter Seven.*

The abundance of similarities between logotherapy and Judaism are not reason to equate the two, or to dissolve the one into the other. This would be a disservice to both, a compromise of uniqueness in both instances. At the same time, the similarities are too great to be dismissed as coincidental and inconsequential.

Chapter Five

LOGOTHERAPY:
ITS RELEVANCE FOR JEWISH THOUGHT

Id, Ego, and Superego are familiar terms to any student of the behavioral sciences. Besides being psychological constructs, they also relate quite pointedly to the developmental aspects of Viennese psychotherapy. The first Viennese school of psychotherapy is, of course, Freudian psychoanalysis, which, in Freud's own words, relates to the basement of the edifice. The second Viennese school is that of Alfred Adler and the third Viennese school of psychotherapy is Viktor Frankl's logotherapy.

Freud and the Id, Adler and the Ego, Frankl and the Superego—these seem to suggest, on a superficial level at least, an evolutionary pattern in the Viennese circle.

In Frankl's words, Freud's system may be broadly characterized as emphasizing the will to pleasure, Adler's the will to power, and logotherapy the will to meaning. Logotherapy, as the third Viennese school, does not reject the contributions of Freud and Adler, but rather sees itself as the dwarf standing on the shoulders of the giant, who is therefore able to see even further. Logotherapy takes the human being as is, without reducing human behavior to id or ego expressions. Instead, logotherapy is a system which asserts that the primary motivational force in the human being is the striving to find meaning in life. Logotherapy is a clinical approach which tackles problems of dis-ease, existential despair, "noogenic neuroses" and even certain forms of depression, by opening up the world of meaning for the patient. Logotherapy's clinical approach is based on a distinct philosophical attitude and approach to the human being.

II

Most Talmudic students who are exposed to Frankl's writings, most notably *Man's Search for Meaning,* feel intuitively that what he has to say is consistent with Jewish tradition.

Such was my reaction about nine years ago, when I first read Frankl's works. I took a chance and wrote a letter to Frankl, briefly describing how his logotherapy seemed to be consistent with Jewish thought. I ended by saying that though we were separated by the Atlantic Ocean, if he ever came over, I would like to meet him.

I received a response quite quickly in which Frankl told me that he would be arriving at a specific date in Rochester. I geared myself for travelling to Rochester on the appointed day. Two days before the anticipated meeting, I received a phone call, person to person, from Boston. It was Dr. Frankl on the line. He had come a few days earlier and would, in fact, be in Rochester not in two days, but tomorrow.

I was overwhelmed by his consideration, having had just token correspondence with him and not even having a firm appointment. I suggested the possibility of my going to Rochester to meet him and he said he was busy and would not have more than five minutes. I took a chance and the five minutes became four hours.

One really cannot appreciate Frankl's philosophy until one sees Frankl, the man. He breathes every word of his theory. He is a living embodiment of the search for meaning and the passionate commitment to bringing the concept of meaning into primariness.

Ironically, for reasons that defy explanation, Frankl has not felt at home amongst Jewish audiences. He relates that when he delivered a lecture to a group of Jewish scholars, they tried to just finish him off, simply because they were against his philosophy and felt that everything had to be explained along Freudian lines. Frankl felt that for this group Freud was higher than Moses—first was Freud and then, let's see to what extent Moses can be compromised with Freud. When he lectured at the Hebrew University, Frankl felt more lonely than when he walked through the desert the previous day.

Other faith systems have eagerly digested logotherapy, which makes his cool reception in Jewish circles even more incongruous.

III

Frankl is an optimistic man. He also looks upon human experience very positively. Having lived through the concentration camps, he is still able to say, on countless occasions, that he prefers a world in which Hitler is possible to a world in which everyone is programmed to automatic goodness. For Frankl, evil is a necessary component for a world that is based on free choice. If only the good is possible, then there are no choices.

It is well known that Frankl went through the concentration camps. What is less well known is that he had an opportunity to leave Vienna. The American Consulate had already called him to receive his visa. But Frankl hesitated because his parents would remain in Vienna and he wanted to stay with them. He noticed a piece of marble lying on the table at home. His father told him that he had found it at the site of the largest Viennese synagogue, which the Nazis had destroyed. It was part of the tablets containing the Ten Commandments. The part that Frankl's father had taken contained just one commandment, the one to honor one's father and mother. Frankl saw this as a call to stay with his parents upon the land, and so he let his American visa lapse.

In Auschwitz, Frankl was forced to surrender his clothes together with a manuscript which was the first version of his book, *The Doctor and the Soul: An Introduction to Logotherapy*, published later on, in 1955, in translation, by Alfred A. Knopf. In exchange for his clothes, he was given the rags of an inmate whom the Nazis had already sent to the gas chamber. He found in a pocket a single page from the Hebrew siddur (prayer book), including the *Shema*, containing in it the obligation to love God with all of one's heart, soul, and might. Or, as Frankl interpreted it, "the command to say 'yes' to life, despite whatever one has to face, be it suffering or even dying."

This incident helped Frankl to overcome the loss of his spiritual child, his manuscript. A life whose meaning would stand or fall over the inability to publish a manuscript would not be worth living. Instead, this single little page took the place of the many pages of his manuscript. It was a symbolic call to Frankl to live his thoughts, instead of simply putting them down on paper.

In the camps, he found corroboration of his conviction that human beings have the freedom to choose. He saw human beings reduced to animals and he saw saints. He saw a living refutation of Freud's thesis that if a number of strongly differentiated human beings are subjected to the same level of starvation, the increasing imperative need for food will blot out all individual differences and they will be replaced by the uniform expression of the one unsatisfied instinct. The concentration camps proved this to be untrue. They corroborated Frankl's view that human beings, at all times, can choose, if not their destiny, the attitude they take toward their destiny.

IV

In fact, Frankl offers a very interesting approach to the problem of free will versus determinism. Rather than apologize for the fact of determinism and its apparent denial of freedom, Frankl twists it around. In an almost Talmudic exercise, he says that freedom without destiny is impossible, that a person may be free but is not floating freely in airless space. There are always restrictions, but they are not contrictions, rather jumping off points for freedom. Freedom is contingent upon restrictions.

Frankl, here, takes the problem and makes it the solution. There is an underlying thought process in all of Frankl's thinking, which is based on the fundamental assumption that humankind must have been granted the means to actualize humanness and that if freedom is necessary to make this actualization possible, it must perforce exist. It is an optimism about life and faith in life's meaningfulness.

In true existential fashion, Frankl makes of other problems solutions. Death is necessary as it points to the human being's finiteness. If individuals could live forever, they would constantly postpone the demands of the day with the valid argument that there will always be a tomorrow. Thus, death is necessary as an existential alarm clock. It is somewhat akin to the Talmudic dialectic in which a sage advised his disciples that they repent one day before their death. They immediately reacted with the obvious question, "how do we know when we will die?" to which the sage responded that is was all the more reason for them to repent today, lest they die tomorrow, and thus their entire life is spent in repentance.[1]

Because individuals are finite, they cannot bridge the gap to the infinite. In an existential sense, this means that the individual is guilty, but guilt implies a sense of responsibleness, for if an individual is not responsible, guilt is impossible. Since individuals have free will, they are responsible and therefore guilty.

Frankl says that the individual has a *right* to be considered guilty and guilt is a healthy aspect if used positively. He has ventured into such unlikely places as the San Quentin prison to impart this notion, and has found a receptive ear amongst the inmates, who resent the usual approach of visiting psychiatrists telling them it is not their fault; they had a bad family foundation or poor environment. It makes the inmates feel their families or environment should be imprisoned, not they. Frankl told them—man is free to become guilty but he is also responsible to overcome guilt. So, they felt responsible for the past, and thus, answerable in the present and open to a more responsible future. This seems to be a logical approach based on some interesting research, which has shown that criminals, as well as alcoholics and drug addicts, usually have low scores on the Purpose-in-Life Test, devised by James C. Crumbaugh to measure the individual's meaning direction in life.

V

Frankl aims to rekindle responsibleness, and hence, responsiveness to the world of meaning and purpose, initiating a process whereby the convict can transcend criminality into the human sphere.

We all desire to be perfect. Frankl insists that we should always desire perfection, but we should be aware of the impossibility of attaining it. Perfection would destroy individual uniqueness, as all individuals would be equalized by the common ground of perfection. It is nuances of individual imperfections which make for the uniqueness of the individual. The individual who is perfect is no more becoming, no more reaching for the world of values. As Frankl would say, as soon as one appreciates one's own sense of finiteness, one thereby overcomes it.

The human being is unique in the capacity to commit suicide consciously and intentionally, as opposed to an animal, which may kill itself, but does not do so through an act of will. What does this mean? It means that precisely because the human being can say no to life through suicide, the decision to remain alive is, in itself, an affirmation of life. The possibility of suicide is a necessary contingency for life's meaningfulness.

We normally tend to think of activity as the way to escape boredom. For Frankl, it is not activity which exists to escape boredom, rather boredom exists in order to show us the meaning of activity. If a sense of emptiness did not creep into an individual who was unfulfilled, there would be no orientation towards finding a meaning.

VI

In logotherapy, the mediating principle between the subject and object, between the human being and the values waiting to be actualized, is the *will to meaning*. The individual does not have a drive towards meaning, rather meaning is willed.

It is a decision, not an urge. Even a religious urge is not a valid and authentic expression. It must be a human choice and the will must be towards meaning, not towards pleasure. In Frankl's view, the will to pleasure is self-defeating in that "the more one aims at pleasure, the less one can attain it." This elusiveness of pleasure is obvious in the famous Midrashic statement that nobody departs from the world with half the desire gratified. One who has one hundred wants to make it into two hundred and one who has two hundred, wants to turn it into four hundred.[2]

Frankl thinks that the will to power is equally self-defeating; the more one strives for prestige, the less one can gain it. It is akin to the Talmudic idea that from one who seeks greatness, greatness flees, but one who flees from greatness, greatness follows.[3] Even self-realization, in Frankl's view, is elusive if sought for directly; self-actualization must come on its own, in the same way that pleasure comes from the fulfillment of a meaning or the living of love.

As a matter of fact, an overwhelming percentage of potency problems in the clinical situation come because one or both of the partners in a relationship are more interested in their own highs than in fulfilling the partner. The Masters and Johnson technique of deflecting the partners from sex was long ago—in fact, in 1947—anticipated by Frankl.[4] Those who seek pleasure have a frustrated sense of meaning. This is evidenced from studies which have shown quite conclusively that the existential vacuum or sense of meaninglessness is much higher in samplings of population that are found in an amusement park. Logotherapy tackles the immediate problem at its philosophical roots, and focuses on the meaning in the relationship to get it back on the right track.

VII

Logotherapy posits the notion of the unconditional meaningfulness of life in any and all circumstances. Even if "creative or experiential values" are rendered impossible by a specific predicament, "attitudinal values" are still possible. The attitude one takes to suffering can give that very suffering a meaning, can change "suffering from" to "suffering towards." Life is not a quantity. It is rather a quality, and it is a quality that only becomes manifest through the human ingredient, what one gives to life. The human ingredient is the commitment to the world of values and meanings.

Frankl insists that is invalid to ask what one can expect from life. Instead, he says, in a German book published in 1946, we should become aware that life is expecting something of us; in other words, that we have to respond to life. The rewards of life are commensurate with what the individual gives to it, or "according to labor is the reward."[5] If life is a quality, its worth cannot be measured in terms of individual achievement of a material nature or the attainment of high position. Life's worthiness is measured by what the human being gives to it. A gas station attendant's life can be much more meaningful than the life of a big-time surgeon. As the Talmud states, one may acquire eternity in a single hour while another may acquire it after many years,[6] each doing one's thing in one's own unique way.

Human achievement is a permanent part of life. It cannot be erased. It is there. As the Talmud says, "All your deeds are written in the book."[7] Why should an individual envy a young person with a life full of potential when in fact potential actualized is of much greater value. The past, in Frankl's words, is one's real future. He approximates the famous Midrash[8] about the ships—the one coming into port and the other going out. The one coming in is congratulated for having achieved its mission. The one that is leaving does so with a sense of trepidation, not knowing what the future holds. Values fulfilled are life lived. As Frankl teaches, only the possibilities to fulfill a meaning are transitory; once, however, they have been actualized, these possibilities have been made into realities, and—in the past—these realities remain forever.

VIII

Frankl's philosophy is obviously quite useful for individuals whose despair is rooted in a distorted philosophy. To be sure, logotherapy carefully avoids imposing values in a clinical situation, but it does not "shrink" from proposing values in the meta-clinical context. Mainly, logotherapy attempts to open up the world of meaning in the patient. Meaning in life is viewed as the corrective for what Frankl terms the "existential vacuum," or sense of emptiness directly linked to lack of purpose and meaning. The so-called "Sunday neurosis" and "unemployment neurosis," as well as perhaps "retirement neurosis," are areas where the existential vacuum are likely realities.

Logotherapy appears as a highly idealistic world-view and clinical approach, but Frankl insists it is not idealistic, but realistic. This, because logotherapy does not moralize about what is right; rather, it develops its view of life from the frame of reference of the healthy human being and healthy human living and translates this into philosophical and clinical terms. This contrasts with other systems which focus on the sick aspects of the person and develop their world-views from that starting point. For logotherapy, the truth about the human condition is perceived in direct relationship to the person's healthy and truly human expression. Logotherapy is, at once, empirical and naturalistic.

Frankl is realistic enough to recognize that "humane humans are, and will probably always remain, the minority." True to form, Frankl sees this less as a reason for despair and more as "a challenge to join the minority."

IX

Frankl is a deeply religious man. He believes there is a religious sense that is deeply rooted in all people. He sees religion as an individual's search for ultimate meaning, a meaning which Frankl insists exists unconditionally, even after Auschwitz. In this widest sense, he thinks, every human being has unconscious religiousness.

What does Frankl mean by unconscious? He states that the foundation of existence cannot fully be reflected upon and cannot be aware of itself. The human spirit in its origin is unconscious spirit. Conscience itself is the voice of transcendence. Unconsciousness is understood as a latent relation to the transcendence inherent in human beings.

The irreligious person is not one who does not have the transcendental quality, rather one who does not recognize it. In Frankl's view, the pathos of atheism is based on an implicit religious ethos and the passion of the unreligious includes a hidden love of God. This is Frankl the philosopher, not Frankl the clinician. Clinically he makes it quite clear that the logotherapist cannot impose religiousness. To genuine religiousness, the individual cannot be "driven by an instinct, nor pushed by a psychiatrist." However, if the issue of religiousness arises in the clinic, the logotherapist is not allowed to negate it, as it is a very positive human phenomenon.

Frankl once recommended to an individual suffering from obsessional neurosis, who had become suicidal, that he stop fighting the neurosis and since the patient was a religious man, Frankl was able to recommend that he see the neurosis as the will of God that should be accepted. The patient's religiousness allowed for such a mediating concept. He stopped fighting the obsessional neurosis and eventually the obsessional neurosis stopped fighting him.

Frankl's philosophy, theology, and clinical theory take an affirmative attitude to the religious quest. In a certain sense, the logotherapeutic view of religion is even more affirmative than some of religion's most zealous practitioners. The fact that logotherapy has much in common with Judaism does not necessarily mean that it is totally consistent with it. One thing, however, is sure. Frankl has supplied the Jewish philosopher, the Jewish theologian, and the Jewish clinician with much to think about.

Chapter Six

LOGOTHERAPY AND TALMUDIC JUDAISM

Any attempt to correlate logotherapy with some religious group or set of religious ideas is fraught with difficulty, mainly because of the dimensional gap which indicates that logotherapy, as a psychotherapy, and religion work from incommensurate frameworks. Frankl's rightful insistence that logotherapy is a secular theory and practice only accentuates the problem.[1] Nevertheless, because logotherapy straddles the border between medicine and religion, it has attracted the theological attention of many religious groups.

II

Logotherapy begins with the basic notion that "the striving to find a meaning in one's life is the primary motivational force in man."[2] This notion is complemented with the philosophical proposition pervading Frankl's writings to the effect that life itself possesses unconditional meaningfulness in all situations, including suffering and the specter of death.[3] This meaning is objective; that is, it is real and always present. But what is meant or implied in the concept of unconditional meaning? Unconditional meaning, even with the objective meaning idea, remains a mystical concept that, although not out of bounds for the secularist, is enticingly attractive for the religious person. Its attractiveness to Judaism can be seen in Leo Baeck's identification of life task with "Torah," the essence of Jewish life and thought. Baeck also was wont to call logotherapy *"the* Jewish psychotherapy."[4]

Beyond the notion of meaning itself, man's adherence to life because of meaning is made possible by faith in meaning, in both existential and ultimate contexts. Ultimate meaning is the macrocosmic aspect on which all the microcosmic, individual meanings lean. Faith in ultimate meaning is not restricted to the religionist, but ultimate meaning as a viable concept invites the religious man to embrace at least the spirit of logotherapy.⁵ It is only a step from faith in ultimate meaning to faith in the Architect of this ultimate meaning, faith in God. A careful reading of Frankl's work indicates that what he means by calling logotherapy a "secular theory and practice" is that logotherapy is *also* secular, that is, open to the secularist as well as the religious man.⁶ Frankl feels compelled to maintain this "secularity" in order that logotherapy may be open to all, and, perhaps, because the concepts in logotherapy border so closely on religious tenets.

This essay explores logotherapy's openness to Judaism; it does not attempt to link logotherapy specifically to Judaism, but to illustrate a basic congeniality between the two disciplines. It will focus on the talmudic explication and extension of biblical thought.

III

Freedom of will, a major philosophical tenet of logotherapy, assumes that man, under all conditions, remains free to choose, although within psychological, biological, and sociological limitations. Freedom toward value actualization is vital if we are to affirm man's capacity to search for meaning and realize values. In a general sense, this is consistent with the biblical approach to man. Although the Bible is replete with exhortations and commandments, talmudic exegesis indicates that punitive measures are instructive, but rarely, if ever, carried out. The biblical approach only serves to accentuate man's freedom to decide, else he could not be considered culpable. Responsibility stems from the fundamental human freedom to choose the direction of one's behavior. "Everything is foreseeen, but freedom of choice is given"⁷ is the talmudic summation of this idea.

The will to meaning, as man's central motivating force, points to the self-defeating nature of the pleasure principle as an indication of its philosophical emptiness. The more a person pursues pleasure, the more it eludes him.⁸ Or, in Midrashic terms, "nobody departs from the world with half his desire gratified. If he has a hundred he wants to turn them into two hundred, and if he has two hundred he wants to turn them into four hundred."[9] Also, the will to power mistakes the means for the end itself; power is a means toward man's fulfillment.[10] The Talmud introduces the futility of quest for power with the assertion: "From him who seeks greatness, greatness flees, but [to] him who flees from greatness, greatness follows."[11] The will to meaning is what logotherapy proposes as the higher principle guiding life. Man is not driven to meaning; rather he wills it.[12] A talmudic counterpart to this notion may be found in the exhortation, "Let all your actions be for the sake of the name of Heaven."[13] Man should will toward that which is meaningful in the religious sense, toward all that is implied in the term "Heaven."

The meaning of life, the third tenet in the logotherapeutic spectrum, stresses the unconditional meaningfulness of life. Frankl introduces three categories of value through which meaning can be found: creative, experiential, and attitudinal.[14] In an interesting aside, he compares the Judaic idea of Shabbat, the seventh day as a rest day, with experiential values. Work on six days is in the realm of creativity, but on the seventh day man finds meaning through experience, through what the word bestows upon him rather than on what he contributes to the world.[15] The attitudinal values, the stance man takes toward his unavoidable predicament, are close in import to the unconditional faith in God, in spite of all circumstances, that pervades Jewish teaching. Man is obliged to manifest his faith in life, in God, even at death's door, "even though He takes your soul."[16] Even when creative and experiential values are no longer possible, attitudinal affirmation of faith remains as a value expression.

Meaning of suffering. Frankl tackles the problem of the ubiquity of suffering head on. He asserts that life is meaningful in spite of suffering, and even goes so far as to say that the "right kind of suffering—facing your fate without flinching—is the highest achievement that has been granted to man."[17] It is easy to affirm life when things go well. The challenge for man is to continue in life even when fate takes bad turns. Were man to give up when confronted by pain, or a crisis, many lives would have been lost, many ideas stifled, and many achievements never realized. The right kind of suffering, that is, not masochistic but necessary suffering, is a human achievement, for it is only human volition that urges man in the suffering situation. In this sense the talmudic statement, "he who joyfully bears the sufferings that befall him brings salvation to the world,"[18] is a complement to Frankl's thoughts.

Quality of life. Logotherapy questions a set of values that would consider a doctor better than a gas station attendant.[19] In essence, man's life is not measured, in human terms, by productivity, material gain, or the headline factor of his profession. Man's life is a quality measured by the human ingredient inherent in that life. The meaningful life of a gas station attendant who works for the sake of his wife and children is superior to the meaningless perfunctoriness of a great surgeon who is primarily out for profit and status. Not what man takes from life but what he gives in answer to the challenge of his existence determines the value of life. Thus, "one may acquire eternity in a single hour, another may acquire it after many years."[20] One need only recall logotherapy's position on the importance of attitudinal values to see how the notion of the quality of life is consistent with the matter of attitudes.

Self-transcendence. Man is seen as one who wills, not one who is driven. Man is not motivated by the need to give off excess energy, or by the homeostasis principle. He *wills* toward a world of values, and actualizes his own self not by intending self-actualization, but tangentially through the process of "self-transcendence."[21] Man strives for values for the sake of those values. He directs his life toward the world rather than toward his self. Frankl himself refers to the statement of Hillel, "but if I am for my own self only, what am I?"[22] and comments, "The question, What am I if I do it for my own sake only, requires the answer: In no event a truly human being. For it is a characteristic constituent of human existence that it transcends itself, that it reaches out for something other than itself."[23] Being oriented around values is the attitude both Frankl and the Talmud consider essential to the human endeavor.

Life as a task. According to logotherapy, it is not for man to confront life. In reality, life confronts man, eliciting from him the proper response consistent with his situation. Each man, in his own uniqueness, finds his way toward the meaning of his life actualized through his task. It matters little whether he performs much or little, as long as he performs his task, as he honestly sees it, to the best of his abilities and responsibleness. Man is a finite creature who cannot bridge the gap to perfection. Thus, "it is not incumbent upon you to finish the task, but neither are you a free man to desist from it."[24]

Responsibleness. Man, once he comes to grips with his own finiteness, with the idea that he need not conquer the world but only fulfill his own obligations, can then make the choice of what values he will actualize. Because he is unique, because each moment unused is wasted, and because he is doomed to death, man is a responsible being. "Human responsibility, which existential analysis strives to make men aware of, is a responsibility springing from the singularity and uniqueness of each man's existence. Man's existence is a responsibility springing from man's finiteness."[25] Every man is a world in whole; the unique character of each individual denies man the cop-out of leaving things to others. Were man a machine, he could legitimately expect any other machine to do as well as he. As a human being, his contribution and role cannot be taken over by anyone else. And, according to the Talmud, "every person is obligated to say: The world was created for my sake."[26] In line with logotherapeutic thought, this talmudic statement posits the vital role of each individual, as if on the shoulders of each person rests a global and untransferable responsibility.

Existential vacuum. In the course of filling one's life with values, man at times comes to grips with the crisis of meaninglessness when, for instance, he stops working and does not know how to find meaningful leisure activities. The ensuing unemployment or retirement neurosis stems from an existential vacuum, an inner void that forges itself out of the emptiness of one's condition.[27] Of course, given the notion of unconditional meaningfulness, a commitment to the meaningfulness of life can only enhance the posibility for rehabilitation of the frustrated retiree. In psychological terms, the statement "idleness leads to idiocy"[28] is a recognition of the ill effects of such a vacuum. In theological terms, "the Holy One, blessed be He, desired to make Israel worthy, therefore he gave to them the Torah [Written and Oral Law] to study and many precepts to fulfill,"[29] a statement pointing to the action taken in Judaism to prevent this self-same existential vacuum from developing.

Unconditional love. In speaking of the love relationship, Frankl affirms the notion of unconditional love, a mutually transcending love that is not contingent on what one or the other partner has, but on what the partner *is,* and still can *become.* It is a union of beings that even transcends death. It is timeless and imperishable. The prototype of this relationship is espoused through the following observation: "All love that depends on a thing, when the thing ceases, the love ceases, and all love that is not dependent on a thing will not cease forever."[30]

The past as future. Because love is seen as transcending death, as imperishable, it cannot fade away into nonexistence. Frankl goes even further when tackling the problem of the transitoriness of life. He provides philosophical and clinical solace to the patient who thinks he has no future: "The only transitory aspects of life are the potentialities; as soon as we have succeeded in actualizing a potentiality, we have transmuted it into an actuality and, thus, salvaged and rescued it into the past. Once an actuality, it is one forever. Everything in the past is saved from being transitory. Therein it is irrevocably stored rather than irrecoverably lost. Having been is still a form of being, perhaps even its most secure form."[31] In carrying through this notion to its logical conclusion, Frankl asserts: "This leads to the paradox that man's past is his true future. The dying man has no future, only a past. But the dead 'is' his past. He has no life, he is his life. That it is his past life does not matter; we know that the past is the safest form of existence—it cannot be taken away."[32] Logotherapy uses this approach to heal the wounds of the aged, telling them they have actualities whereas the young only have potentialities. This approach finds a parallel in the Midrashic exegesis of the verse "and the day of death [is better] than the day of one's birth."[33] "To what can this be compared? To two ships laden with merchandise sailing the ocean, one coming in and the other going out, and the people praised the one coming in. Some people stood there and wondered: 'Why are you praising this one and not the other?' They replied to them: 'We are praising the ship that came in, because we know that she went out in peace and has returned in peace. As to the one now going out, we do not know what her fate will be.' Thus when a man is born we do not know what the nature of his deeds will be, but when he departs this world, we already know of what nature his deeds are."[34] Both logotherapy and Judaism agree that past accomplishments are better than future possibilities.

Paradoxical intention. One of the unique features of logotherapy is its projection of specific techniques, including paradoxical intention. While the clinical efficacy of paradoxical intention has already been attested to, a word about its moral and theological implications seems in order.

Talmudic literature presents a number of instances closely paralleling paradoxical intention. Regarding the futile nature of the pursuit of power, the Talmud asserts: "From him who seeks greatness, greatness flees, but him who flees from greatness, greatness follows."[35] The more man intends power or glory, the less likely he is to achieve it. This, of course, is not paradoxical intention in relation to an obsessive-compulsive neurosis, but rather related to man's basic inclinations.

In the philosophical realm, one finds the following dialogue between Alexander of Macedon and the elders of the south city: "He said to them: What shall a man do to live? They replied: He should mortify himself. What shall a man do to kill himself? They replied: He should keep himself alive."[36]

Again, the paradox alluded to here is not clinical, but philosophical. Nevertheless, these examples show an acceptance of the concept of paradox in Judaic thought patterns in a way anticipating the Kierkegaardian notion that truth is perceived in paradox. Paradoxical intention in logotherapy is more than a technique. The concept of paradox pervades logotherapeutic thought. Thus suffering gives meaning to life, guilt is a positive force in the human endeavor, imperfection is needed in the human situation, boredom is a useful tool to avoid the existential vacuum, man's past in his true future, etc. As the rabbis turned life on its head, logotherapy accentuates the positive by turning the aspects of suffering, guilt, death and boredom paradoxically into meaningful realities.

In a specific area, however, paradoxical intention poses a problem. The Talmud relates of a scholar, Rav, that he was tormented by his wife. If he asked for lentils, she would give him small peas; if he asked for small peas, she would give him lentils. When Rav's son Hiyya grew older, Rav transmitted his wishes through him. Hiyya reversed his father's instructions, so that Rav now got what he wanted. Rav remarked to Hiyya that his mother had improved; Hiyya admitted that it was only because he had reversed the orders that Rav's wishes were fulfilled. Rav, in admiration, acknowledged that he had been taught a lesson by his offspring, yet he asked his son to discontinue the practice, since he would be teaching his tongue to lie.[37]

Again, the situation is not a classic case of paradoxical intention, as it deals with solving a material dilemma rather than alleviating a neurosis. However, the external features are strikingly similar. The warning Rav gave his son seems pertinent here. What if, for example, paradoxical intention is used to heal a neurosis with religious overtones? By telling the patient to intend the very thing his religious principles instruct him to avoid, one might cure the neurosis, but at the price, potentially, of an inconsistent, if not troubled inner consciousness. To illustrate, if the patient with a neurotic fear that he might desecrate the Sabbath is told, in paradoxical intention, to make up his mind that he will desecrate the Sabbath not once, but a hundred times, we may heal the neurosis but in the process break his ideals, as he now wills what his faith teaches him to avoid. He teaches himself to lie.

These illustrations are not intended to disparage logotherapy. If any psychological system has gone out of its way to accommodate the religious dimension, it is logotherapy. The point that issues from this brief discussion is that paradoxical intention can, in certain instances, create a greater problem than the one it solves. Frankl indicates that paradoxical intention does not work for everyone.[38] The devoutly religious man who cannot even think of breaking the rules is, like the museum guard, an unlikely candidate for paradoxical intention. Strangely, if not typically, logotherapists would be the first to admit the difficulty and refuse to compromise the patient's religious principles, for clinical as well as spiritual reasons.

IV

In this essay I have taken the piecemeal approach, amalgamating various individual though interrelated concepts. I have not exhausted the areas of common thought, but merely tried to indicate the vast areas of common concern and expression shared by the two systems.

What is the purpose of the entire exercise? Surely Judaism remains little affected by being compared to logotherapy. As a religious system that has survived centuries of tragedy, it does not need any crutch. At the same time, logotherapy as a system open to all spheres of thought can sustain itself without reinforcement by Judaic thought. Yet in the long run, there are benefits. Judaism can openly embrace a psychotherapy that is philosophically consistent with its own affirmation and can even evolve a logotherapeutic approach to the problems that are indigenous to it. Logotherapy is in a small measure enhanced by the obvious congeniality it has with faith, in particular with the faith of Judaism, the oldest existing religion of the Western world. But beyond this is a larger, more imposing development. Frankl has on many occasions averred that logotherapy, based as it is on some of the oldest concepts, is not so much novel as it is neglected in the spiritual malaise that plagues the world today. While we are surprised at the many notions Frankl turns upside down, in the Eastern cultures his paradoxes are already well known, if not taken for granted. Logotherapy, then, is but a return to the sources of life itself. Its correlation with Judaism, itself a primary affirmation of life, serves to illustrate the fact that logotherapy is a return to the pristine beauty of life. The uniqueness of logotherapy, then, is not in its newness, but in its timelessness. That, ultimately, is its greatest asset.

Chapter Seven

LOGOTHERAPY AND JUDAISM— SOME PHILOSOPHICAL COMPARISONS

The luck of the draw, pot luck, and other forms of good fortune have been traditionally associated with Las Vegas, Bingo parlors, race tracks, etc. More recently, the projection of various personages on the world stage as giants of the spirit has been exposed in many instances as gross misrepresentation, if not distortion. Even the supposed choosing of a President is acknowledged to be more a matter of being in the right place at the right time, a fusion of the many necessary facets of luck, than it is a matter of possessing the talents and qualities for the job. One speaks of the "making" of the President, rather than the "choosing" of a President.

It would be expected that in the world of the intellect, the realm of scholarship, the element of luck should not be a factor. Ideas and issues should here be judged on objective grounds, without intervention of elements extraneous to the subject matter. Scientific objectivity and all that it implies militates in this direction. However, such is not always the case. Witness the differing reactions by Jews to Sigmund Freud and his Psychoanalysis in contrast to Viktor Frankl and his Logotherapy. Freud was accosted, even embraced by his Jewish brethren, even though he declared:

> The Jewish societies in Vienna, in short the Jews altogether, have celebrated me like a national hero, although my service to the Jewish cause is confined to a single point—I have never denied my Jewishness.[1]

Frankl, on the other hand, has been virtually ignored. Not only have Christians who studied logotherapy ignored his relationship to Jewish tradition, but he is also almost unknown in contemporary Jewish thought. Frankl's relative obscurity in Jewish circles cannot be dismissed as an accident. He writes of an experience when lecturing a group of Jewish scholars:

> I gave a lecture and they just tried to finish me off. Everybody was against my philosophy and said it is clear that everything has to be explained along the lines of Freudian psychoanalysis; because Freud is to this Jewish group higher than Moses; first comes Freud, and then let us see to what extent Moses can be compromised with Freud.[2]

Frankl writes further:

> I have lectured at the Hebrew University in Jerusalem. On the day before, I went through the desert, until I did not see anything but desert. The next day when I was lecturing on Logotherapy at the Hebrew University, I felt more lonely than when I was in the desert.[3]

All this, even though Frankl makes no pretenses about his Jewishness, and adheres, in his personal life, to much of the Jewish tradition. For reasons which must belong in the domain of *mazzal,* luck, Frankl the Jew has not been accepted by his brethren, whilst Freud the Jew has been accepted. What effect this has had on the prominence of Freudian psychoanalysis as opposed to the obscurity of Franklian logotherapy in Jewish circles is a matter of conjecture. Suffice it to say that the responsibility for objectivity demands a closer examination of logotherapy in the light of Jewish tradition. "Frankl, the man and his philosophy, deserves greater recognition and a wider audience."[4]

This essay will present the basic philosophy which underlines logotherapy as a clinical tool, and will propose some comparisons of this philosophy with traditional Jewish thought. It should be noted at the outset that what is being suggested is not an equating of logotherapy with Judaism. The dialectic of Judaism on the issues which will be discussed is too variegated to identify the "Jewish" view. It will suffice to present some common ground shared by logotherapy and Judaism.

Logotherapy, the teachings of the third Viennese School of

Psychotherapy, is a psychotherapy which derives its tenets from the essence of man's spiritual dimension.

> Man lives in three dimensions: the somatic, the mental, and the spiritual. The spiritual dimension cannot be ignored, for it is what makes us human.[5]

As opposed to the Freudian school, which centers on the will to pleasure, and the Adlerian school, which focuses on the will to power, this movement concentrates on the will to meaning. The kernel of the logotherapeutic thesis may be summed up in the following: "The striving to find a meaning in one's life is the primary motivational force in man."[6] Logotherapy attempts to understand man relative to the meaning of his existence. It concerns itself with the problems of meaninglessness, the "existential vacuum," and the resultant noogenic neuroses. Joseph Fabry has translated logotherapy as "therapy of meaning."[7] As an aside, Frankl refers to Leo Baeck's translation of Torah as "meaning," and sees a common direction shared by logotherapy and Judaism.

Frankl asserts that every form of clinical psychotherapy is based on a philosophy of man, a philosophy which is at times covert. "Every school of psychotherapy has a concept of man, although this concept is not always held consciously."[8] Frankl's logotherapy is, of course, no exception to this rule. Fortunately, the philosophy espoused by logotherapy is fundamentally explicit. The concept of man which serves as the foundation of logotherapy consists of three fundamental, interrelated assumptions: (1) freedom of will; (2) will to meaning; and (3) meaning of life.

II

According to Frankl, man possesses a positive vector, a natural bent towards an objective goal in transcendent space. Frustration of this natural inclination may lead to what Frankl has termed "noogenic neuroses."[9] Freedom of will is seen as the absence of any factor which impedes man's flight into noetic space. Three forces in and around man are generally regarded as constricting in this sense: instinct, inherited disposition, and environment.

With regard to instincts, Frankl asserts;

> Certainly man has instincts, but these instincts do not have him. We have nothing against instincts, nor against a man's accepting them. But we hold that such acceptance must also presuppose the possibility of rejection. In other words, there must have been freedom of decision. We are concerned above all with man's freedom to accept or reject his instincts.[10]

Concerning inherited traits, Frankl counters that predisposition is an indication rather than a negation of freedom. He cites the evidence of identical twins who evolve differently from the same predisposition.

> Of a pair of identical twins, one became a cunning criminal, whilst his brother became an equally cunning criminologist. Both were born with cunning, but this trait in itself implies no values, neither vice nor virtue.[11]

Accordingly, the difference between the criminal and the criminologist is basically a difference in how each decides to parlay his cunning.

Frankl takes a parallel approach with regard to the environment factor. All depends on what man makes of his environment, on his attitude toward it.[12]

Instinct, heredity, and environment become, in Frankl's view, partial and potential determinants. They are partial determinants in that they establish the specific boundaries of human behavior. Within these limits, man is free to decide what his stand will be. These factors are potential determinants in that man can accept, reject, or manipulate them according to his own volition. He possesses the ability to rise above the bounded surface area of psychic and somatic determinants into a new, distinctly human dimension, the spiritual, or noological. Floating in this dimension, man can look down at the forces which tend to dehumanize him, and ultimately he alone decides the extent to which he will be steered by them. In the noological domain, man exercises the distinctly human phenomenon of self-detachment, detaching his self from himself and becoming the arbiter of his future.

Frankl is not concerned with the reality that biology may confine man's vocational choice or that sociology may dictate it. As long as man, within a given framework, remains able to ascend the heights which are indicated by his humanity, as long as he retains the ability to actualize values, he is considered free. This stems from the implicit notion throughout Frankl's writings that freedom is interrupted only by factors which prevent man's natural bent to reach specific values. Frankl believes that no such factor exists, for with the potential of a determining factor is necessarily attached the ability to reject it. Frankl goes so far as to consider man's destiny, or his conditional factors, as prerequisites for freedom:

> Freedom without destiny is impossible; freedom can only be freedom in the face of a destiny, a free stand toward destiny. Certainly man is free, but he is not floating freely in airless space. He is always surrounded by a host of restrictions. These restrictions, however, are the jumping-off points for his freedom. Freedom presupposes restrictions, is contingent upon restrictions. . . .
>
> The ground upon which a man walks is always being transcended in the process of walking, and serves as ground only to the extent that it is transcended, that it provides a springboard.
>
> If we wanted to define man, we would have to call him that entity which has freed itself from whatever has determined it (determined it as a biological-psychological-sociological type); that entity, in other words,

that transcends all these determinants either by conquering them and shaping them, or by deliberately submitting to them.[13]

In a word, Frankl admits the existence, even the necessity, of horizontal restrictions, but denies the existence of vertical restrictions. Man is conceived as having positive vertical vector, to be impeded by horizontal factors only as much as he allows.

Freedom, for Frankl, demands no special proof. It belongs "to the immediate data of his experience."[14]

Freud once said:

> Try and subject a number of very strongly differentiated human beings to the same amount of starvation. With the increase of the imperative need for food, all individual differences will be blotted out, and, in their place, we shall see the uniform expression of the one unsatisfied instinct.[15]

The concentration camps, in Frankl's view, proved Freud wrong. The camps proved that man cannot be reduced to a function of heredity and environment, for at the same time that some inmates of the camp degenerated into the innate camp bestiality, others exhibited the virtues of saintliness. A third variable, found only in the spiritual animal, man, is the decisive factor in human behavior, choice or decision. "Man ultimately decides for himself."[16]

The experiences of the concentration camps as proof of man's free will demand further explanation. Is not the skeptic likely to claim that those who behaved as bestially as their environment were compelled by conditions? As for the exceptions who attained saintly status, perhaps they possessed saintly instincts. Why derive from the few that man is free when the actions of the many indicate he is not?

The response to this is that freedom of the will, in Frankl's view, is not a necessary component of behavior, but a potential to be realized;

> For in every case man retains the freedom and the possibility of deciding for or against the influence of his surroundings. Although he may seldom exert this freedom or utilize this opportunity to choose—it is open to him to do so.[17]

Man will be shaped by his environment as long as he does not pause and confront himself with life. Man becomes free the moment he detaches his self from himself and analyzes the meaning of his life vis-a-vis where life is carrying him, or the moment he becomes human. The prisoner of biology, sociology, or psychology is ultimately the man who has allowed these forces, by his passivity, to impede his humaneness.

The notion of free will as developed by logotherapy invites some interesting comparisons. Because logotherapy is conceived as a secular discipline, the problem of free will vs. Providence is extraneous to the logotherapeutic framework. The theological ingredient in Judaic free will is lacking in logotherapy, so that any comparison must make dimensional adjustments.

Sforno, commenting on the words ". . . He formed him in the likeness of God,"[18] explains this as meaning man is master of choice. Free will is here seen as a Divine ingredient in man. The ultimate resolution of the free will vs. Providence problem appears to be a matter of faith. The Talmudic recognition of this problem comes in the form of a succinct statement stating the problem whilst at the same time using the problem as the solution. "Everything is foreseen but the right (of choice) is granted."[19] The solution is the problem itself. All is foreseen, but not in a causative manner. God's foreknowledge and man's free will are not mutually exclusive. There is no attempt in this statement to solve the dilemma. Rather, it tends toward the idea that faith in God as the all-powerful and all-knowing Creator is what gives life purpose, what gives man faith in his own existence. Having faith in meaningful existence and in purposeful creation are inseparable concepts, and, as faith, have value in spite of seeming incomprehensibility. Without free will, however, life itself loses meaning, so that meaningfulness, and faith in same, are predicated on free will. Logotherapy too, which postulates the notion of the unconditional meaningfulness of human existence, has as its first philosophical principle the existence of free will.

The Franklian notion of freedom as dependent on destiny is a striking parallel to the Talmudic statement "everything is in the hand of heaven except the fear of heaven."[20] Rashi, in elaborating, explains that whether a man is tall or short, poor or rich, wise or stupid, depends on pre-destination; the only choice left for man is whether he will be righteous or wicked.

As the logotherapist would interpret it, man's environment, his social condition, his biological makeup, are of necessity predetermined, but the attitude of man to his condition remains untouched by determinism. His social condition may prevent him from attaining certain vocational objectives, his biological makeup may restrict his social development, but no factor impedes man in his quest to realize meaning in his life situation.

Frankl's reference to the twins with cunning, one of whom became a lawyer, the other a criminal, has its parallel in the following Talmudic passage;

> He who is born under Mars will be a shedder of blood. R. Ashi observed: Either a surgeon, a thief, a slaughterer, or a circumciser.[21]

The mazzal man is born under, his destiny, is not a negation of the idea of free will. According to logotherapy, man's freedom can only be understood in the face of some destiny.

III

The second major philosophical tenet of logotherapy is the will to meaning.

Pleasure and power, the fulcrums of life according to Freud and Adler, are undermined by Frankl. At no time does he moralize against these principles. His outlook towards them is an outgrowth of life experiences. Frankl, here and throughout his works, creates a unique form of experiental philosophy, combining his experiences as a doctor and concentration camp inmate with his existentialist leanings. He establishes as a yard-stick the properly functioning human being, function here taken in an existential sense. Life's goals and aspirations are judged according to their utility in attaining and maintaining proper functioning. The will to pleasure, for Frankl, "is a self-defeating principle inasmuch as the more a man would really set out to strive for pleasure the less he would gain it."[22] Moreover, most cases of sexual neuroses are resultant of striving directly for pleasure. In healthy reality, pleasure is merely a byproduct of fulfillment. The will to power is really the tools manipulated by man in order to achieve some goal. There is a higher principle guiding life, the will to meaning.

> In the last analysis, it turns out that both the will to pleasure and the will to power are derivatives of the original will to meaning. Pleasure, as mentioned above, is an effect of meaning fulfillment; power is a means to an end. A certain amount of power, such as economic or financial power, is generally a prerequisite of meaning fulfillment. Thus we could say that the will to pleasure mistakes the effect for the end; while the will to power mistakes the means to an end for the end itself.[23]

Frankl is not hereby denying that man aims for pleasure or power. That such striving is the underlying cause of certain neuroses leads Frankl to reject them as absolute goals in a properly functioning human being; the properly functioning human being serving as the model, or construct, of Frankl's philosophy.

The striving to find a meaning in one's life has been categorized by Frankl as *will* to differentiate from *drive*. Man is not driven toward meaning, for then his behavior would be symptomatically equivalent to the homeostatic urge involved in the pleasure principle. Meaning would lose meaning, and would become a tool through which man satisfies his desire for equilibrium.

Then, too, *will* admits of choice, whereas *drive* implies an irresistable inner force compelling behavior. Freedom of will is the necessary philosophical forerunner of the will to meaning.

Meaning as a drive would also not fit into Frankl's implicit system of man as positive vertical vector. Satisfying drives have as their ultimate purpose the relaxation of the tension caused by them. But tensionless man is directionless man, and directionless man is bound to develop those neuroses that are born of directionlessness, or boredom, or, as Frankl calls it, the existential vacuum. It is thus rejected as drive and established as will on the grounds that as a drive it would not be conducive to the human model.

Even self-realization and self-actualization are seen as side effects of man's search for a meaning outside himself:

> The true meaning of life is to be found in the world rather than within man or his own psyche, as though it were a closed system. By the same token, the real aim of human existence cannot be found in what is called self-actualization. Human existence is essentially self-transcendence rather than self-actualization. Self-actualization is not a possible aim at all, for the simple reason that the more a man would strive for it, the more he would miss it. For only to the extent to which man commits himself to the fulfillment of his life's meaning, to this extent he also actualizes himself. In other words, self-actualization cannot be attained if it is made an end in itself, but only as a side effect of self-transcendence.[24]

Frankl adds a new component to his human model. Man is

perceived as positive vertical vector of infinite magnitude. Self-transcendence is a never-ending dynamic, just as life and meaning. Man is always striving; one accomplishment is not an excuse to relax from the responsibilities facing man, is not an end in itself. Self-actualization would perhaps set a limit to the human vector, inviting through the suspension of dynamics some form of neurosis.

Accomplishment becomes the momentum for additional accomplishment, and in this perpetual process man fulfills, tangentially, his own self.

Frankl's rejection of the pleasure principle as it is self-defeating has some interesting parallels in Talmudic literature. According to Norman Salit, the self-defeating nature of the striving for pleasure

> is in the nature of the motivation that appears in a similar maxim in the Talmud: "From him who seeks greatness, greatness flees; but him who flees from greatness, greatness follows." The real saints were those who sought not sainthood but service.[25]

The formula as stated by Frankl that the more a person sets out to strive for pleasure the less he will gain it, is more clearly alluded to in the following:

> Nobody departs from the world with half his desire gratified. If he has a hundred he wants to turn them into two hundred, and if he has two hundred he wants to turn them into four hundred.[26]

The idea of the will to power as a means rather than an end is clearly congenial to the Judaic view, which places so much responsibility on the man with means, and calls the various forms of charity *tzedakah*, implying that sharing wealth is just and equitable, not philanthropic. The power gained through wealth becomes the means through which to actualize the meaning values entailed in possession.

Frankl proposes the will to meaning as the primary motivational force in man. One senses almost intuitively that the term "meaning" employed by Frankl is closely akin to what the Talmud intends with the term "Torah." Thus, the statement "every man is born for toil"[27] is explained as meaning "that one was created to labor in the Torah."[28] Torah becomes the vehicle for meaning.

The affinity the basic thrust of logotherapy has with Judaic cosmology invites the following observation:

> What Frankl calls "Logotherapy" and the "will to meaning" is not unlike the striving for an ordered, meaningful cosmos on the part of the rabbinic teachers in their own times.[29]

Frankl insists that the essence of the human endeavor is self-transcendence. We now call upon Frankl himself to illustrate how the notion of self-transcendence relates to Judaism. Frankl, in alluding to the statement of Hillel, ". . . but if I am for my own self (only), what am I"[30] expounds:

> What here comes in is no more nor less than the self-transcendent quality of human existence. The question, What am I if I do it for my own sake only—requires the answer: In no event a truly human being. For it is a characteristic constituent of human existence that it transcends itself, that it reaches out for something other than itself.[31]

Frankl delineates sharply between the concept of self-transcendence and the notion of self-actualization, calling self-actualization a side-effect of self-transcendence rather than a primary phenomenon. This recalls the Talmudic dictum "make them not a crown wherewith to mignify thyself, nor a spade wherewith to dig,"[32] which can be interpreted in the logotherapeutic vein as: Do not make Torah, the transcendent value system, a crown, a vehicle for self-actualization. Meaning must be pursued for its own sake, *lishmah;* the self-realization follows naturally.

IV

The third major philosophical tenet of logotherapy is the *meaning of life*. As opposed to the concepts of freedom of will and will to meaning, which are approached on phenomenological grounds, Frankl's concept of the meaning of life is a little more abstract.

Logotherapy conceives of man as one who wills. To conceive of man as one who wills, as one who is "pulled by meaning,"[33] is to conceive of a world filled with objective meaning. Frankl stands in rigid opposition to the homunculist, nothing-but picture of man; man portrayed as biology-sociology-psychology; the subject, man, being reduced to an object, or accident, of his conditions. Concurrently, Frankl rejects the subjectivization of all values, the reduction of meaning to mere self-expression. Man, like the decrepit arc, needs a pulling tension, a subject-object dynamics, or, in Frankl's words, noodynamics:

> Cognition is grounded, indispensably, on a field of polar tension between the objective and the subjective, for only on this basis is the essential dynamic of the cognitive act established. I call this dynamic "noodynamic" —in contrast to all psychodynamics.[34]

Man oscillates between the subjective "I am" and the objective "I ought," and insofar as he strives for the ought he transcends his self and actualizes his responsibleness. In Frankl's view, "existence falters unless it is lived in terms of transcendence toward something beyond itself."[35]

The subject, man, is thus confronted with objective values. These values pull him, eliciting from him the noodynamic reponse which willfully transcends the subjective state into the objective value world.

Frankl offers no proof that objective values exist. That these values are objective follows necessarily from Frankl's view of man. The human model, the properly functioning man, is directed towards meaning. If meaning were subjective, the dynamics of transcendence would be destroyed and existence would falter. Therefore, meaning must be objective. No circular argument, this principle as well as others in Frankl's system are derived from the premise that truth is perceived in utility. Man is at his best when indulging in self-transcendence, thus testifying to the validity of the concept of self-transcendence. Since self-transcendence demands objective values, objective values are as real as existence, the tools needed to achieve his mission in life.

In Frankl's notion of objective values is salient an unshakeable faith in the unconditional meaning of existence. It is this faith in unconditional meaning which is the hallmark of logotherapy. The three basic philosophical tenets of logotherapy are emanations from this faith. Meaningful existence means that man *chooses* his existence, and is not driven to choose but rather *wills* his choice. The choice, however, is resultant of a confrontation with *objective* values. Man decides whether to say yes or no to these values.

There is, according to Frankl, no general, all-encompassing meaning of life. It is comparable to the question posed to a chess player, "What is the best move?" There is no best move just as there is no universal meaning. Instead, meaning is detected in man's confrontation with his unique situation. Every man is unique, all situations are unique, hence all confrontations are unique. Each confrontation carries its own particular meaning; man detects the objective meaning in the subjectiveness of his situation.

Frankl does categorize three species of values contained in life. They are (1) creative values, or what man gives to life; (2) experiental values, or what man takes from the world in terms of his experience; and (3) attitudinal values, or the stand man takes toward an unchangeable aspect of his existence.

Attitudinal values are central to logotherapy, for they are directly linked to the concept of unconditional meaningfulness. Frankl insists that even when man is choked by tortuous suffering, he can still exercise his humaneness.

> Thus, life has a meaning to the last breath. For the possibility of realizing values by the very attitude with which we face our unchangeable suffering—this possibility exists to the very last moment. . . .[36]

Man's life is judged not on a quantitative basis, but on what he makes of his life situation, a qualitative judgment. The meaningful question is not "what," but "how," not what was accomplished, rather how was life lived, how were the singular opportunities that total man's existence used?

> It is not from the length of its span that we can ever draw conclusions as to a life's meaningfulness. We cannot, after all, judge a biography by its length, by the number of pages in it; we must judge by the richness of the contents. The heroic life of one who has died young certainly has more content and meaning than the existence of some long-lived dullard. Sometimes the "unfinisheds" are among the most beautiful symphonies.[37]

In the suffering situation, the range of choice is naturally constricted, but attitudinal choices are still available. That man cannot choose to travel to a country which can use his talents because he is bedridden does not mean he is not free. The constrictedness of his situation gives birth to unique objective values which form the matrix of his choice options. Freedom itself is only meaningful in the face of values which confront man.

Frankl's notion of objective values again strikes a close parallel with the Judaic notion of values embodied in Torah.

> What is the meaning of the verse: *"And I will give thee the tables of stone, and the law and the commandment, which I have written that thou mayest teach them?"* *'Tables of stone:'* these are the ten commandments; *'the law:'* this is the Pentateuch; *'the commandment:'* this is the Mishnah; *'which I have written:'* these are the prophets and the Hagiographa; *'that thou mayest teach*

them:' this is the Gemara. It teaches (us) that all these things were given to Moses on Sinai.[38]

This Talmudic passage is a statement establishing the value code of Judaism as given at revelation. Revelation is the handing down of the tools of the human dynamic, values, to humankind. The objectivity of values is established through its emanating from a source outside the subject, man. The path of Frankl's insistence on objective values approximates, within the secular dimension, the theological thrust of Judaism.

In Judaism, man is confronted with the unique value set which encompasses Torah. The concept of *tinok shenishbah,* the child who is taken into captivity, and is thus not blamed for his non-adherence to Judaism, may be seen as based on the absence of a confrontation with Judaism. The captive child has never had a chance to say "yes" to Judaism, and his non-adherence is therefore not considered saying "no" to Judaism. Ideally, the Jew's choosing of his faith is the outgrowth of his confrontation with that faith, what logotherapy would call a subject-object dynamics. However, when the subject is denied encounter with the objective, the resultant vacuum cannot be ascribed to him.

Judaism too, does not prescribe any set, rigid path to human existence. Whether one is a sage or a laborer, "from the hewer of thy wood unto the drawer of thy water,"[39] man can carve a niche for himself in the encounter which is life. The vital factor is: "let all thine actions be for (the sake of) the name of Heaven,"[40] that is, the actions should be oriented in the transcendent meaning direction.

Frankl's distinction between creative and experiental values finds its expression in Judaism. Again, we call on Frankl himself to illustrate:

> Meaning can be found in life . . . for six days by working. But . . . work is not the only task we have—literally man was not made only to labor. That is to say, the meaning of Shabbat may well consist in reaching

beyond work. There are creative values, there are experiental values, there are attitudinal values. This means we may find the meaning in our lives through a deed we are doing, through a work we are creating, through an achievement and accomplishment, through creativity, six days. But also through our experience. Not through what we give to the world but what we receive from the world; what we take in.[41]

The attitudinal value concept and its importance in facing suffering again invite comparison with the anecdote reported in the Talmud when R. Eliezer fell ill. Three elders tried to comfort him by praising him and his great deeds. The fourth, R. Akiba, startled him with the simple declaration, "Suffering is precious."[42] R. Akiba explained his statement through an allusion to a particularly evil monarch who was unmindful of all attempts to reform him but was brought back on the right path through suffering. Man's proper attitude to his suffering makes suffering precious. Indeed, "he who joyfully bears the chastisements that befall him brings salvation to the world."[43]

It goes almost without saying that Frankl's approach to life on a qualitative rather than quantitative basis is congenial to Judaic thought. Although there are such ostensibly quantitative maxims, as "everything is in accordance with the preponderance of (man's) deed(s),"[44] yet the feeling that life is a qualitative entity persists. "One may acquire eternity in a single hour, another may acquire it after many years!"[45] Quantity yes, but qualitative quantity.

V

This essay has attempted to show how the philosophical foundations of logotherapy relate to Judaism. At this point, I am not prepared to say that everything in logotherapy is an expression of Jewish tradition, or is even compatible with Judaism. What can be asserted without hesitation is that there is enough reason to believe that a dialogue between Judaism and logotherapy is possible, if not imperative.

It is true that Frankl conceives logotherapy as a secular theory. Yet this secularity is not intended to cut off the religious dimension. It is a secularity in the form of religion for the non-religious, an attempt to make logotherapy available *even* to the atheist and agnostic. This openness of logotherapy leads into many theological areas, including Judaism.

> Consciously or unconsciously, Frankl has given expression to traditional Jewish concepts and insights; his Logotherapeutic approach to the ills of the human psyche are consistent with the basic tenets of Judaism.[46]

Those who feel the need to develop a Jewish psychotherapy need not resort to dubious creativity when a system which is apparently open to Judaic thought and is acknowledged for its clinical efficacy is available. One can at this point in time only echo the feeling that insofar as logotherapy is concerned, it has been almost ignored by its most logical advocate. This is unfortunate for both, as Judaism and logotherapy can only gain from a direct confrontation with one another.

SECTION 4

CONFRONTING DEATH

PRELUDE

Long before contemporary society became obsessed with the matter of death, logotherapy devoted much attention to the fact of death in life. The spirit of optimism and positive attitude to life as espoused by logotherapy are illustrated in *Chapter Eight*. The positive attitude is operative even in the face of one's mortality.

Chapter Nine takes a more detailed look into the fact of death and how it can translate into a more meaningful life. Both chapters contain further comparisons with some Jewish views on these matters of concern.

What evolves is a deep appreciation of the affirmative stance toward life which is basic to logotherapy.

Chapter Eight

REFLECTIONS ON PAST AND FUTURE

The two words characteristic of the most prevalent human moods are *hope* and *despair*. Hope, an optimistic frame of mind, is generally associated with the future; *despair* by contradistinction is a sense of future*lessness,* either because of the feeling of emptiness that no future can rectify, or because of the inevitableness of death.

Existentialism, focusing on the here-and-now of woes and predicaments, has popularized numerous pessimistic terms, such as dread, sickness unto death, nausea, anxiety, crisis, etc. Although identified with existentialism, logotherapy, the analytical method developed by Viktor E. Frankl, is unique in its optimistic approach to life. Logotherapy is future-oriented. It emphasizes hope and meaning rather than despair. It accentuates the positive of future promise and not past failure.

Judaism, too, is future-oriented. It knows that while humans are finite and imperfect, and therefore liable to err and sin, we are also capable of self-perfection to a certain degree. Judaism does not explain sinfulness as a "spur of the moment reaction," "haphazard occurrence," or an act caused by "temporary insanity." Indeed, the Talmud asserts that *"a person does not sin unless a spirit of folly (shetut) enters into him,"*[1] but this is not intended to condone misbehavior or punishment. Rather this talmudic statement is expressive of Judaism's optimism. If one sins, it is because some foreign ingredient—a spirit of folly—has taken possession of him. As Judaism sees it, if transgressors want to mend their ways, they need only divest themselves of "the spirit of folly" and return to their selfhood.

One of the Hebrew terms for sin is *averah,* derived from a root meaning "to pass" and linked to "the past." It is not overindulgence in homiletics to equate the Jewish concept of wrongdoing with the past; that is, sin, after being committed, is a thing of the past which need not determine the future. Judaism rejects the notion that sin constitutes an eternal burden of guilt, that one's future is doomed because of the past. Repentance *(teshuvah)* can erase the past if implemented by good deeds in the future. This conviction is expressed as follows:

> If you see a scholar who has committed an offense by night, do not cavil at him by day, for perhaps he has done penance. 'Perhaps,' say you?—Nay, rather, he has certainly done penance.[2]

Even if we have witnessed wrongdoing, we should assume that the wrong has been righted and that, as a result, the past has been deprived of power. We can always mend our ways:

> Even if one has been completely wicked all his life but repents at the end, he is not reproached for his wickedness.[3]

I have heard many, almost hostile, reactions to this talmudic passage. It is not right, it is argued, that a rascal should get away with last minute repentance. But the Sages referred to *sincere* repentance. The Sages refused to concede that the human situation is ever hopeless. Retrievement is always possible. There is no hopeless situation.

II

Viktor Frankl sets the same optimistic tone in logotherapy. He stresses that the endeavor to find meaning in life is the primary human motivation. Frankl insists there is always meaning in life—to the very end. He does not acknowledge the inevitableness of the consequences of inherited dispositions or environmental coercion. He emphasizes the human ability to exercise free choice despite circumstances, and asserts that we can surmount any and every situation. As proof he cites the many, including himself, who retained hope and trust in meaning in the Nazi death camps.

Logotherapy focuses on the future, both in the clinical and meta-clinical situations. In Frankl's words:

> But man cannot really exist without a fixed point in the future. Under normal conditions his entire present is shaped around that future point, directed toward it like iron filings toward the pole of a magnet.[4]

In the Nazi concentration camp, Frankl tried to alleviate the despair of fellow-sufferers by finding some task in the future that called upon their inner resources. He challenged those who despaired to struggle and survive in order to fulfill that future task. Frankl never lost faith and hope, and he instilled that faith and hope in some of his fellow prisoners. Logotherapy asserts that man can bear suffering if he can see beyond it, however remotely, into the future. This insight is based on Frankl's own experience.

But there are situations when finding a meaning seems futile. But even then, Frankl writes, "A human being, by the attitude he chooses, is capable of finding and fulfilling meaning in even a hopeless situation."

The faith in the unconditional meaningfulness of life enables one to elicit a positive response in all situations. Thus, a nurse suffering from a terminal illness was told that her attitude to pain would go a long way in helping the many patients in her care. This give her a meaning in suffering.

Facing death is the main challenge to the meaning-orientation of logotherapy. It is the sorrow and agony of the person who is facing his end, as well as of those who suffer a tragic loss. In trying to meet this challenge, logotherapy is compatible, if not consistent, with Jewish thought.

> Actually, the only transitory aspects of life are the potentialities; as soon as we have succeeded in actualizing a potentiality, we have transmuted it into an actuality and, thus, salvaged and rescued it into the past. Once an actuality, it is one forever. Everything in the past is

saved from being transitory. Therein it is irrevocably stored rather than irrecoverably lost. Having been is still a form of being, perhaps even its most secure form.[5]

Frankl therefore concludes:

This leads to the paradox that man's past is his true future. The dying man has no future, only a past. But the dead 'is' his past. He has no life, he is his life. That it is his past life does not matter; we know that the past is the safest form of existence—it cannot be taken away.[6]

There is a parallel to this approach in a Midrashic exegesis of *and the day of death (is better) than the day of one's birth*.

To what can this be compared? To two ships laden with merchandise sailing the ocean, one coming in and the other going out, and the people praised the one coming in. Some people stood there and wondered: 'Why are you praising this one and not the other?' They replied to them: 'We are praising the ship that came in, because we know that she went out in peace and has returned in peace. As to the one now going out, we do not know what her fate will be.' Thus when a man is born we do not know what the nature of his deeds will be, but when he departs this world, we already know of what nature his deeds are.[7]

Here, as in Frankl's thought, there is a balanced attitude to the future. While both Judaism and logotherapy concern themselves with the manifold possibilities of the future, they do not become obsessed with it. After all, is not every future moment destined to become part of the past? Past accomplishments are always better than future possibilities. On this logotherapy and Judaism are agreed.

III

Logotherapy extends its affirmative attitude also to aging. Our culture's glorification of youth has induced fear of aging and envy of the young. Frankl writes:

> Even in advanced years one should not envy a young person. Why should one? For the possibilities a young person has or for his future? No, I should say that, instead of possibilities in the future, the older person has realities in the past—work done, love loved, and suffering suffered.[8]

Logotherapy insists, as Judaism does, that even in the twilight of life man should not stop working and being active. The inability to do one's best in later years need not deter a person from trying. Here, too, the delicate balance between future promise and past accomplishment must be maintained. In his positive attitude to the past, Frankl also points to solace for the individual who has experienced a tragic loss.

> Imagine what consolation the logotherapeutic attitude to the past would bring to a war widow who has only experienced, say, two weeks of marital bliss. She would feel that this experience can never be taken from her. It will remain her inviolable treasure, preserved and delivered into her past. Her life can never become meaningless even if she might remain childless.[9]

Indeed, memory is transient. Frankl properly asks who will keep the memory alive after the widow dies. He thinks that an appropriate response is the following:

> To this one may answer, it is irrelevant whether anyone remembers or not; just as it is irrelevant whether we look at something, or think about something, that still exists and is with us. For it exists regardless of whether we look at it or think about it. While it is true that we can't take anything with us when we die, the totality of our life, which we have lived to completion and death, remains outside the grave, and outside the grave it remains. And it remains not although, but because, it has slipped into the past and has been preserved there.[10]

The concept of a deed *remaining in the world* raises questions about the meaning of existence proper. Frankl comments:

> Now it is my contention that man really could not move a limb unless deep down to the foundations of existence, and out of the depths of being, he is imbued by a basic trust in the ultimate meaning. Without it he would have to stop breathing.[11]
>
> This ultimate meaning necessarily exceeds and surpasses the finite intellectual capacities of man; in logotherapy, we speak in this context of a supra-meaning.[12]

Frankl takes the daring step of suggesting that this world may not be the ultimate reality.

> For all that man may occupy an exceptional position, for all that he may be unusually receptive to the world, and that the world itself may be his environment—still, who can say that beyond this world a superworld does not exist? Just as the animal can scarcely reach out of his environment to understand the superior world of man, so perhaps man can scarcely ever grasp the superworld, though he can reach out toward it in religion—or perhaps encounter it in revelation.[13]

Frankl's concept of a "supra-world" is, I suggest, a synonym for *olam haba*—the world-to-come.

Logotherapy has a perspective of time totally differing from the time concepts of philosophy and psychology. The future is potential fulfillment and, moreover, it is extended beyond existence as we know it. Frankl has an elastic approach to time, which extends the future into the past as well as into a supra-world. The broad ramifications of logotherapy's meaning-orientation encompass all of life from past reality to all future posibilities.

Chapter Nine

DEATH IN LIFE—TALMUDIC AND LOGOTHERAPEUTIC AFFIRMATIONS

In spite of all the sophistication of a highly technologized 20th century, man has essentially still not come to grips with the psychologically traumatic and emotionally enervating experience of death. To be sure, one finds the odd intellectual or the odd man-in-the-street who is philosophical about death, who is ready, so to say, to live with death. In the main, however, the average man still fears death, the process of dying, and the experiencing of death. Perhaps it should be this way. Perhaps it is ridiculous for philosophers and psychologists to attempt pseudo-explanations which explain, even explain away, death. Perhaps it is the height of obscenity to reduce what is assuredly an awesome reality into an acceptable experience. Then, too, it is possibly self-contradictory for man to, at one and the same time, glorify life and accept death. After all, if life is so valuable, and human existence so beautiful, death should be avoided. And, even though death cannot be avoided in fact, it can be avoided in mind. Taking into consideration man's preoccupation with life, it is to be expected that thoughts of death should be suppressed. The thought of death having been suppressed, man becomes psychologically unequipped to face death when death confronts him.

If what we have said is true, then the secularized 20th century technology as a creeping philosophy does not enhance, rather it exacerbates the problem. Man's cold and calculated sophistication, designed to mediate between man and nature in a this-worldly setting, almost totally ignores what may be called "the ultimate problems of man's being." The concerns of a dubious tomorrow are muted in the obsessive preoccupation with today. And, as long as death and what follows death are relegated to the "tomorrow," the "today" world will find it increasingly difficult to properly understand death.

What is needed to deal with the problem on a meta-clinical level is an acceptable philosophy of life which fuses together the today and tomorrow, a philosophy which goes beyond the "as if" of a Camus but is more livable than the *sein-zum-tode* of a Heidegger. If the today and tomorrow can be shown to be intermingled and intertwined, then perhaps the philosophical problems of death can be tackled. The hope is that the psychological aspect would follow.

II

In attempting to formulate a philosophy of life and death to deal with the aforementioned problems, the present paper will present two traditions, one religious, the other secular, relating to the role of death in life. The religious tradition is that found in the Talmudic and Midrashic literature of Judaism. The secular tradition is the logotherapy of Viktor E. Frankl.

Even a cursory glance at the legislative structure of Judaism indicates an appreciation for life. With few exceptions, man is, in Judaism, at all times excused from the performance of a commandment when this endangers his life.[1] Danger to life suspends the code of Jewish existence. According to some,[2] this does not even allow man the possibility of being a theological hero. He must suspend religious observance for the higher reality, life itself. At the same time, the atttitude to death in Judaism is a surprisingly positive one. Midrashic comment on the verse "and God saw everything that He had made, and behold, it was very good" (Genesis 1:31) suggests that "very good" can be equated with death.[3] In a similar vein, it is said of the psalmist David that "He looked upon the day of death and broke into song."[4] At once, we are thus confronted with an affirmative attitude to life and a positive outlook to death. In simple terms, the two ideas can be reconciled with the mediating principle that man would not be faced with an imperative to act and accomplish if his life were endless. That his existence may be terminated suddenly is a reality which forces, or should force, man to utilize his allotted moments as meaningfully as possible.

It seems, though, that awareness of death in the abstract is not deemed enough to act as imperative. Thus, to prevent transgression, the Talmud proposes that man be mindful, among other things, of where he is eventually going, to a place of dust, worms, and maggots.[5] Of the righteous it is said that they "set their death in the forefront of their thoughts."[6] And a famous sage, to bring home the importance of awareness of death, suggested to his disciples that they repent one day before their death. Immediately he was confronted with the expected question, does then man know on what day he will die? To which the sage responded, "Then all the more reason that he repent today, lest he die tomorrow, and thus his entire life is spent in repentance."[7] Repentance here is presented in the existential sense, as the constant process of investigating the past to improve the future. In any event, we have here an ancient thought system which correlates the fact of death with meaningful life. Admittedly, there is a danger in proposing an extreme such as constantly being mindful of death, which can easily give birth to neurotic behavior. It would be more realistic to take this extreme as a counter to the extreme of neglect, with man in his own unique situation striking a delicate balance. The balance might rest in the awareness of death when establishing the "game-plan" for life, and in investing one's life energies in carrying out the plan.

The paradoxical nature of man's relation to death is best expressed in a dialogue between Alexander of Macedon and the elders of the south city.

> He said to them: What shall a man do to live? They replied: He should mortify himself. What shall a man do to kill himself? They replied: He should keep himself alive.[8]

A Midrashic counterpart of the same is the following: "Death is near to you and far from you, as well as far from you and near you."[9] The more man is interested merely in keeping himself alive the more he cuts himself off from meaningful living. In the pursuit of years he wastes the days. The more man realizes he is mortal, destined to die, the more he will try to accomplish, thus perhaps even gaining immortality. Basic to the Talmudic approach is the inherent notion that death, properly understood, can be a vital life force. Needless to say, the element of fear can easily enter into the religious sphere, as when man is urged to behave in life because of the consequences he might face afterwards. Such a confrontation with life and death out of fear, which might yield positive results on a quantitative level, nevertheless falls short on the qualitative level. To propose transcending death in an atmosphere of fear is to circumvent the trauma of death with an even greater dis-ease, the life lived in fear. An affirmation of the role of death in life on an existential level would thus seem to be most appropriate. For this, we turn to the existential philosophy underlying the logotherapeutic system of Viktor E. Frankl.

III

Logotherapy is the school of psychotherapy fathered by Frankl and focusing on the importance of meaning in life. Logotherapy proposes the existence of unconditional meaningfulness and posits the notion that man's primary motivational force is to find meaning in life.[10] Logotherapy, unlike other existential systems, is basically an optimistic, future-oriented system, focusing on man's freedom and the multitude of possibilities for man to find meaning. Logotherapy carefully avoids injecting such ideas as fear, trembling, sickness-unto-death, nausea, anxiety, etc., into the human situation. Instead, ideas such as hope, meaning, joy, ecstasy, and values form its basic lexicon. Nevertheless, logotherapy does not recoil from facing squarely the issues of suffering and death.

The process of death, according to Frankl, is not a severed fragment of the human biography. Death is part of life. "Without suffering and death human life cannot be complete."[11] In projecting the notion of "unconditional meaningfulness," man is called upon to elicit meaning up to and including the moment of death. For "human life, under any circumstances, never ceases to have meaning, and this infinite meaning of life includes suffering and dying, privation and death."[12] The thesis of logotherapy is that man is to live, and die, meaningfully.

So much for the moment of death. What bearing does the inescapability of death have on life itself?

Frankl believes the fact of death is crucial to life; "only in the face of death is it meaningful to act."[13] Contrary to the thought that death indicates the futility and meaninglessness of life, Frankl asserts that if man's life tenure were really infinite in duration, he could continually, and legitimately, postpone every action forever. It would not really matter whether a deed was performed now, or ten years from now. "But in the face of death as absolute finis to our future and boundary to our possibilities, we are under the imperative of utilizing our lifetimes to the utmost, not letting the singular opportunities—whose 'finite' sum constitutes the whole of life—pass by unused."[14] In a word, man exists in time and time exists in man. In the becoming process, the man-time combination is utilized. The death of man in time signifies the passing of a life. The death of time in man signifies the passing of a moment. Ultimate death is only a more radical form of expiration, more radical than the death in installments involved in the wasting of time.

On the other hand, proper utilization of time signifies a positive irreversibility, for that which has been accomplished remains as a reality forever. Transitoriness applies only to the potentialities, which, once actualized, are, so to say, "rescued . . . into the past."[15] Death poses a constant imperative to man, an imperative which says that each moment, as life itself, is irrepeatable, and must be utilized. Death makes life meaningful. The challenge of life is how to use each moment, which values are to be actualized, and which doomed to nonexistence.[16] In logotherapy this is taken to indicate the importance of the past, that "man's past is his true future."[17] The past deeds are "safely stored," immune from any erasure. And, for the dying man who has no future, the past, which is really his life, is the eloquent testimonial to his existence. Death ends the becoming process. In death man "is" what he was in life.[18]

Ironically, Frankl, to counter the negativism usually linked to the fact of death, actually introduces the ubiquity of death even in life, in the passing of time, as a counter to nihilism. The fact that not only life, but also the moment can be lost, and are in fact irreversible, leads to the logotherapeutic notion of man's responsibleness in life. For, if what has been done can forever be undone, and vice versa, then virtue and vice would disappear in uncertainty, praise and blame would be impossible and education unmanageable. Human beings would be free from the responsibilities which underlie their humanness. Responsibleness is a responsiveness to the challenges posed by life, challenges which call for undelayed response. If the existence of man in time is "temporality" and the existence of time in man is "singularity," the following statement capsules these ideas: "The meaning of human existence is based upon its irreversible quality. An individual's responsibility in life must therefore be understood in terms of temporality and singularity."[19]

Irretrievability of a past moment, singularity, and of a past life, temporality, constitute the basis of human existence, and are the impetus for man's responsibleness to life. Frankl thus sees death as an ongoing life process, not in the pessimistic sense, but in the positive sense. Just as total death, the death of man in time, challenges man's life in its totality, so fragmentary death, the death of time in man, challenges man in each moment. The sum of these moments constitutes the existence of man.

IV

It is instructive at this point to note the striking similarities between the Talmudic and logotherapeutic attitudes to death. Although they are separate systems, the one religious, the other secular, nevertheless both take an affirmative attitude to death. The affirmative attitudes are no doubt born of differing assumptions. At work in the Talmud is the fundamental faith that God would not have put in the world a purely negative reality or fact of life. This is not to glorify or seek death, rather to indicate that death enhances the human situation. In logotherapy one senses an optimism with life which is, at once, a philosophical and psychological proposition. As death is unavoidable, it is psychologically silly and philosophically untenable to deny its importance. And, to avoid the dangers of negativism, which can only impede the human situation, it is vital to say yes to life in its totality. Even if life appears senseless, and death more than meaningless, it is vital for man to make life and death as meaningful as possible, to make life philosophically justifiable and psychologically livable. In both these systems, there is an inherent affirmation of the natural order, and an implicit faith in all life contingencies.

In a sense, one may argue that logotherapy presents nothing new, taking into account the fact that its ideas already appear centuries ago in the Talmud. Then, too, the affirmative attitude to death is already found in the writings of so many existential thinkers. Perhaps the uniqueness of the logotherapeutic approach is that it is so affirming while being a secular system, and is affirming with a positive and realistic bent.

For the man-in-the-street, theological or logical propositions are not likely to evoke any excitement. Theology and philosophy have a habit of finding the ear of few people. If Hegel is correct in saying history is what man does with death, then the 20th century poses a unique challenge. Some see in the proliferating abundance of life-saving techniques and their use on the dying person a denial of the individual's right to his own death.[20] It is almost as if science is doing its utmost to see if it can beat the death force, if it can conquer nature. And, ironically, the same medical prowess which tries to conquer death is the judge of when medicine can no longer help, when the situation is hopeless to the point that euthanasia is indicated. In these attitudes one senses a trend to deny nature, to let medicine prolong, and, if need be, to terminate. The affirmative view of logotherapy is consistent when it asks if "we are ever entitled to deprive an incurably ill patient of the chance to 'die his death,' the chance to fill his existence with meaning down to its last moment."[21] For, "the way he dies, insofar as it is really his death, is an integral part of his life, it rounds that life out to a meaningful totality."[22]

Perhaps what we should be arguing for is a return to nature, to an awareness and appreciation of the natural, unavoidable aspects of human existence. Feifel hints at this when he argues that "the concept of death must be integrated into the self to subdue estrangement from the fundamental nature of our being."[23] Frankl alludes to it when he asserts that "this acceptance of finiteness is the precondition to mental health and human progress, while the inability to accept it is characteristic of the neurotic personality."[24]

In the striving for an orderly, structured world, a world of rules and clear-cut patterns which are undoubtedly necessary for technology to benefit the masses, the matter of death has suffered the fate that is to be expected when eschewing the inevitable.

The ultimate answers relative to the problem are not logical but paradoxical. From the Talmudic dialogue previously cited to the effect that to live one must mortify himself and to die one should indulge in life, to the Heideggerian idea that one can conquer death by actually willing it, to the logotherapeutic notion that to the extent which man understands his finiteness he also overcomes it,[25] it is evident that man magnifies the problems of death by avoidance, and counters these problems by accepting and affirming the role of death in life. In espousing an affirmative attitude to the natural order, it might be possible not only to effectively overcome the trauma associated with death, but also to re-enter into meaningful dialogue with life, and to project human concerns into the forefront of man's endeavors.

SECTION 5

LIVING WITH TRAGEDY

PRELUDE

The matter of suffering is perhaps an even greater challenge than the fact of death. One's mortality can remain an abstract, and the concern about death may be primarily philosophical, but suffering is the immediate experience of pain, anguish, grief. It is a clinical and meta-clinical problem. *Chapter Ten* puts forward logotherapy's unique approach to suffering. Some have haphazardly accused logotherapy of being too preoccupied with the morbid side of life. But it is no trick to affirm the positive when things are going well, and it is no help to blind oneself to the fact that every life properly lived will have some measure of suffering. To offer some intriguing insights into coping with suffering is an enduring achievement. It is, in fact, one of logotherapy's greatest achievements. Paradoxically, through its concern for suffering, logotherapy has supplied the means to transcend the suffering situation.

Chapter Eleven tackles the most agonizing moral dilemma of our times, the holocaust. The holocaust and "unconditional meaningfulness of life" seem to be mutually exclusive, if one is to agree with some reactions to this most bestial display in human history. Frankl offers his own reaction to the holocaust. In a word, the holocaust does not shatter his optimistic approach, and even reaffirms it.

This should not be seen as an abstract judgment. Frankl is himself a survivor of Nazi cruelty, and his stance toward life remains intact even though he saw and experienced the abyss, or perhaps *because* he did.

Chapter Ten

LOGOTHERAPY AND THE TALMUD ON SUFFERING: CLINICAL AND META-CLINICAL PERSPECTIVES

Logotherapy, the unique school of psychotherapy fathered by Dr. Viktor E. Frankl, is a system of life which focuses on the meaning of human existence, the objective reality of meaning, and how the person relates to meaning by searching for it. Logotherapy asserts that "the striving to find a meaning in one's life is the primary motivational force in man."[1]

No one escapes suffering of one form or another. In one Talmudic view, even reaching into the pocket for three coins and only taking out two is considered a Divine visitation of suffering.[2] There are different levels and intensities of suffering, but they usually involve despair, and sometimes even the questioning of life's meaningfulness. Life's meaningfulness cannot be divorced from suffering, even from the meaning of suffering.

According to Frankl:

> If there is a meaning in life at all, then there must be a meaning in suffering. Suffering is an ineradicable part of life, even as fate and death. Without suffering and death human life cannot be complete.[3]

Without an adequate approach to the meaning of suffering, logotherapy itself cannot be complete. Logotherapy posits the notion of the unconditional meaningfulness of life, in any and all circumstances, and must come to grips with the problem of suffering. No one is more aware of this than Frankl himself.

Frankl, in his writings, speaks of three types of suffering. They are (1) the suffering associated with an unchangeable fate, such as an inoperable cancer; (2) the suffering which comes as a result of an emotionally painful experience, such as the loss of a loved one; and (3) the suffering which arises out of the existential vacuum in one's life, through the frustration of one's attempt to find meaning in life.

II

Frankl's concept of suffering is consistent with his concept of the person. The human being is one who strives to find meaning in life by actualizing values, be they creative, experiential, or attitudinal. Life is that form of existence which affords the person the opportunity to realize values and actualize one's essence. The person's human vector receives its force and direction from the meaning of life. If any point in life lacked meaning, it would interrupt the human vector and suspend the dynamics of life. Frankl firmly believes the meaning and dynamics of life are never suspended short of death. Thus, every situation in life has potential meaning in it, even the various experiences of suffering.

Frankl writes:

> But even a man who finds himself in the greatest distress, in which neither activity not creativity can bring values to life, nor experience give meaning to it—even such a man can still give his life a meaning by the way he faces his fate, his distress. By taking his unavoidable suffering upon himself he may yet realize values. Thus, life has a meaning to the last breath. For the possibility of realizing values by the very attitude with which we face our unchangeable suffering—this possibility exists to the very last moment. . . . The right kind of suffering—facing your fate without flinching—is the highest achievement that has been granted to man.[4]

However, Frankl explicity refers to "unavoidable" suffering; that is, a suffering whose cause cannot be erased, otherwise the suffering would be unnecessary, meaningless, and possibly masochistic. Attention is focused on the despair inherent in the suffering, for it is the ingredient of despair which obstructs the positive flow of human life.

In this vein, Frankl asserts:

> With special regard to suffering, however, I would say that patients never really despair because of any suffering in itself. Instead, their despair stems in each instance from a doubt as to whether suffering is meaningful. Man is ready and willing to shoulder any suffering as soon and as long as he can see a meaning in it.[5]

Frankl would not do away with suffering, rather he would erase the negative factor of despair to allow the individual's positive human expression to be actualized.

The Nazi concentration camps of World War II are an indication, according to Frankl, of the importance of meaning in suffering. The will to survive in spite of the unbearable hardship of camp life needed the added will to meaning in order for actual survival to be realized, for this magnified the "will to survive" to an "ought to survive."[6]

It should be noted that we find Frankl arguing here for the meaning ingredient not from any philosophical viewpoint, rather from the view that it is conducive to the human condition and affords the capability to transcend a suffering situation. Truth here seems to be perceived in utility, and this approach is observable also in other areas of logotherapeutic endeavor.

In the seemingly meaningless and futile atmosphere of the concentration camps, meaning could be elicited by giving the prisoner a future goal around which to orient.

> It is a peculiarity of man that he can only live by looking to the future. . . . And this is his salvation in the most difficult moments of his existence, although he sometimes has to force his mind to the task.[7]

The meaning alluded to here is not a meaning to the suffering itself, rather a meaning beyond the suffering, a meaning to be attained only through surviving the suffering. As such, this approach is partially reminiscent of the logotherapeutic technique of de-reflection, in that the persons' thinking is oriented towards an event or task beyond the suffering.

Frankl himself seems to search for the actual meaning of suffering. He recalls that most of the inmates of the concentration camp were concerned with whether they would survive the camp, else all the suffering was meaningless. For Frankl, the question was to be asked in reverse. "Has all this suffering, this dying around us, a meaning? For, if not, then ultimately there is no meaning to survival."[8] Frankl insists, as has been previously mentioned, that there must be a meaning to suffering if there is meaning to life at all, since suffering is a component of life. One's attitude to suffering affords the chance to endow life with profound meaning. The individual may embody the virtues of braveness, dignity, and unselfishness, or may be reduced to bestial behavior. In its positive extension, one realizes values through suffering.

Frankl does not really uncover the meaning of the suffering out of pain. Rather, suffering has been made a tool through which to achieve. It has been given utility, meaning has been attached to it. At most, suffering can be extended to manifest an existential corrective for spiritual myopia. The intrinsic meaning of the suffering would have to be determined by the extent to which a future meaning is made possible by the suffering.

III

The person knows of a suffering which is entirely devoid of physical pain, an emotional suffering which stems from the loss of what was basic to life, such as a parent, spouse, or child. Frankl insists on extracting meaning from every life experience, even suffering born of mourning. He views this suffering as a healthful component of life. "A sense of the meaning of emotional experiences is deeply rooted in human beings."⁹ This is seen in patients who suffer from melancholia anaesthetica, or from the inability to be sad. Using the human model, this would indicate that there is nothing inherently wrong with sadness, or with being sad. Frankl gears himself towards erasing the deflating effect of this type of suffering. He would like to transpose the *suffering from* to a *suffering to*, to raise the person above suffering, to elicit meaning from the suffering. Frankl illustrates his approach with the following example:

> An old doctor consulted me in Vienna because he could not get rid of a severe depression caused by the death of his wife. I asked him, "What would have happened, Doctor, if you had died first, and your wife would have had to survive you?" Whereupon he said, "For her this would have been terrible; how she would have suffered!" I then added, "You see, Doctor, such a suffering has been spared her, and it is you who have spared her this suffering; but now you have to pay for it by surviving and mourning her." The old man suddenly saw his plight in a new light, and re-evaluated his suffering in the meaningful terms of a sacrifice for the sake of his wife.¹⁰

Frankl does not attempt to tranquilize away the pain. Neither does he attempt to reincarnate, in any way, the deceased. He redirects, through a change in attitude, the suffering factor from negative to positive. Suffering becomes a jumping-off point for meaning fulfillment rather than a life-choking experience.

The cynic is likely to question Frankl insofar as his approach to the doctor is concerned. Could not all suffering have been avoided if the doctor and his wife had expired simultaneously? Such a question, however, misses the basic point of logotherapy's approach to suffering of this type. There is no attempt to advance pseudo-theological explications from the predicament. Instead the focus is affixed on the reality of the situation, how best to approach it, and how best to retroactively invest the suffering experience with some meaning. It might be the meaning of sacrifice, as in the case of the doctor; in another case it might be through living the ideals of the departed. Either way, the suffering situation is taken as given, and approached futuristically rather than analytically.

IV

Besides the suffering normally associated with pain or loss, there is a third type of suffering, "a suffering beyond all sickness, a fundamental human suffering, the suffering which belongs to human life by the very nature and meaning of life."[11] This suffering stems from a frustration of the search for meaning, or, as Frankl calls it, the will to meaning. It is reminiscent of the Midrashic observation that "all the time that one increases knowledge, one increases suffering."[12] This type of suffering, the inner tension aroused by the search for values, is seen by Frankl not as a pathological phenomenon, rather as a human achievement, a "positive achievement in the highest sense of the term."[13]

The person who suffers from existential frustration has, by this very suffering, exercised self-detachment. The person has begun to judge reality in terms of capability, or what the individual ought to be. Frankl insists that unavoidable suffering of this type, inherent as it is in the human condition, must be faced realistically. He decries the attitude of many who would tranquilize away the pain by repressing the metaphysical striving.

> The principle of "euphoria at any price" as a motivation for the medical approach must be refuted because "pleasure gain at any price" and "freedom from pain at any price," would be tantamount to partial euthanasia.[14]

Some clarification of this statement by Frankl is in order, to avoid the charge that such an approach borders on sadism. Frankl himself admits that in the suffering crisis of existential maturation "treatment of the covering-up type might be less painful but it also deprives life of much meaning."[15] The question begs itself, how much pain is logotherapy advocating that people endure to actualize meaning? Frankl acknowledges that the existential analyst may sometimes be called on to decide what is and what is not meaningful suffering, whether or not it is of the avoidable type. Yet there is hardly a suffering which cannot be either erased or numbed.

In the final analysis, suffering boils down to a biological-psychological or noological phenomenon. The biological factor, in terms of an irreversible fate, admits of no cure. The noological factor, the mental torment, exists in a different sphere or dimension, the distinctly human sphere Frankl calls the noos (spirit). Frankl welcomes spiritual suffering insofar as narcotic or tranquilic escapism would mean spiritual death, or partial euthanasia. It is when pain and meaning are in the same dimension, the noological, that Frankl insists on sacrificing painlessness for meaning.

It would appear that this type of suffering, existential suffering, is most conducive to uncovering an intrinsic meaning.

> Suffering is intended to guard man from apathy, from psychic rigor mortis. As long as we suffer we remain psychically alive. In fact, we mature in suffering, grow because of it—it makes us richer and stronger.[16]

Undoubtedly, this is a reference to the suffering emanating from an existential vacuum. Nevertheless, this still does not explain the meaning of suffering. One can still grow without the suffering and apathy can still be checked without suffering. Ultimately, the problem of the meaning of suffering can be paraphrased as—"Why is suffering necessary?"

V

For the person of faith, the problem of suffering can be approached on theological grounds. In the words of Max Scheler, quoted by Frankl:

man has a right to be considered guilty and to be punished. Once we deal with man as the victim of circumstances and their influences, we not only cease to treat him as a human being but also lame his will to change.[17]

From this vantage point, the hammer blows of suffering might be seen as necessary insofar as without them the sufferer might shrink into spiritual oblivion. They might be conceived as the intentional rude awakening to the purpose of one's life, to a confrontation with reality. The suffering out of the existential vacuum would then not be real suffering, rather a healthy despair which proclaims, *Do something about it*. In this respect, it might be said that "every man has the right to endure his own kind of suffering."[18]

However, even though the person of faith might be satisfied with such an existential-theological approach to suffering, the problem of meaning is not much better off in this framework. The questions that may be posed to logotherapy can be asked of the theologian, and, perhaps even more acutely. Beyond this, imminence of death and the attendent suffering are situations which almost defy even theological rationalizations. Frankl recognizes the insurmountable difficulty in trying to understand suffering on theological grounds. He asserts:

> No man can really see the necessity of Divine intervention in terms of punishment, because he can never know why God has punished him, or else, why God was gracious enough to spare him punishment; nor why God insists on punishment, because God's reasons cannot be understood by man.[19]

The hallmark of logotherapy is in its espousing the notion of the unconditional meaning of life. Every moment and each situation of existence has potential meaning which can be realized. Logotherapy is deeply sensitive to explicating the dilemma of suffering. Frankl asks:

> Is it not possible that there is still another dimension possible, a world beyond man's world; a world in which the question of an ultimate meaning of human suffering would find an answer?[20]

In reality, finding an ultimate meaning to suffering is as impossible as finding an ultimate meaning to life itself. And, within the framework of logotherapy, the inability to concretize an ultimate meaning of life is conducive to life's dynamics, for if ultimate meaning could be rationally expressed in finite terms, it could then also be achieved in finite time. But reaching such a pinnacle would suspend the dynamics of life, allow for no value realization, and thus divest life of its unconditional meaning. Unconditional meaning implies perpetual striving for the unreachable, the unfathomable, and precludes the possibility of establishing a finite frame of reference for the purpose and meaning of life.

Suffering, which belongs to life, would then fall into the same category as life, and would manifest the same built-in unknowability.

> What is demanded of man is not, as some existential philosophers teach, to endure the meaninglessness of life; but rather to bear his incapacity to grasp its unconditional meaningfulness in rational terms.[21]

Herein is capsuled the paradox of the life dialectic. One strives for what is ultimately unknowable, yet the striving itself would be choked off were it really knowable. This is the paradox of meaning in suffering as well.

Frankl, to be sure, embarks on an approach which wrestles with, but does not quite embrace theology. This results from Frankl's insistence that logotherapy be available for the religious and non-religious alike. He sees religion as a human phenomenon which must be viewed positively in the clinical situation,[22] but at the same time insists that the logotherapist not impose religiousness on the patient, since "to genuine religiousness man cannot be driven by an instinct —nor pushed by a psychiatrist."[23]

The logotherapist must be attentive to the patient's values, and react accordingly. Frankl, when involved in the situation of an eighty-year-old lady suffering from incurable cancer who was becoming increasingly depressed, tried to illuminate, for the patient, the meaningfulness of her life; that her experiences would not be erased and were lasting.

> *Dr. Frankl:* You are speaking of some wonderful experiences; but all this will have an end now, won't it?
>
> *Patient (thoughtfully):*
> In fact, now everything ends . . .
>
> *Dr. Frankl:* Well, do you think now that all of the wonderful things of your life might be annihilated and invalidated when your end approaches? (And she knew that it did!)
>
> *Patient (still more thoughtfully):*
> All those wonderful things . . .
>
> *Dr. Frankl:* But tell me: Do you think that anyone can undo the happiness, for example, that you have experienced? Can anyone blot it out?
>
> *Patient (now facing me):*
> You are right, Doctor; nobody can blot it out!
>
> *Dr. Frankl:* Or can anyone blot out the goodness you have met in your life?
>
> *Patient (becoming increasingly emotionally involved):*
> Nobody can blot it out!
>
> *Dr. Frankl:* What you have achieved and accomplished.
>
> *Patient:* Nobody can blot it out!
>
> *Dr. Frankl:* Or what you have bravely and honestly suffered: Can anyone remove it from the world — remove it from the past wherein you have stored it, as it were?
>
> *Patient (now moved to tears):*
> No one can remove it! *(Pause)* It is true, I had so much to suffer; but I also tried to

be courageous and steadfast in taking life's blows. You see, Doctor, I regarded my suffering as a punishment. I believe in God.[24]

To this point, Frankl has handled the situation within the strictly human dimension. But the patient, through her last comments, has opened up new horizons. Frankl continues:

Dr. Frankl: But cannot suffering sometimes also be a challenge? Is it not conceivable that God wanted to see how Anastasia Kotek will bear it? And perhaps He had to admit: "Yes, she did so very bravely." And now tell me: Can anyone remove such an achievement and accomplishment from the world, Frau Kotek?

Patient: Certainly no one can do it!

Dr. Frankl: This remains, doesn't it?

Patient: It does!

Dr. Frankl: By the way, you had no children, had you?

Patient: I had none.

Dr. Frankl: Well, do you think that life is meaningful only when one has children?

Patient: If they are good children, why shouldn't it be a blessing?

Dr. Frankl: Right, but you should not forget that, for instance, the greatest philosopher of all times, Immanuel Kant, had no children, but would anyone venture to doubt the extraordinary meaningfulness of his life? I rather think that if children were the only meaning of life, life would become meaningless, because to procreate something which in itself is meaningless certainly would be the most meaningless thing. What counts and matters in life is rather to achieve and accomplish something. And this is precisely what you have done. You

> have made the best of your suffering. You have become an example for our patients by the way and manner in which you take your suffering upon yourself. I congratulate you on behalf of this achievement and accomplishment, and I also congratulate your roommates who have the opportunity to watch and witness such an example. . . . I should say, your life is a monument. And no one can remove it from the world.
>
> *Patient (regaining her self-control):*
> What you have said, Professor Frankl, is a consolation. It comforts me. Indeed I never had an opportunity to hear anything like this.[25]

This case is a clear illustration of how logotherapy blends its philosophical foundations with clinical reality, fusing its philosophy of meaning with the patient's religiousness to effect a cure from depression.

VI

Frankl's approach to suffering concerns itself, in the clinical and meta-clinical dimension, with a major theological dilemma.

The Talmudic approach to suffering begins from a different starting point. It sees suffering as an act of God. Unconditional faith in God includes even the situation of suffering and death. To love God "with all your soul"[26] is interpreted to mean "even as He takes your soul."[27] In this framework, even "suffering is precious."[28]

A positive meaning-oriented approach to suffering is encouraged. Thus, one who is visited by painful suffering is urged to examine personal conduct.[29] The suffering is not seen as an accident, and, once inflicted, is seen as a vehicle to elicit meaning through self-investigation and improvement.

Suffering, approached properly, brings one closer to God.

"One should be grateful to God when overcome by suffering. Why? Because suffering draws the person closer to God."[30]

The Talmud espouses a positive attitude to suffering, and its approach travels along the lines of logotherapy's view of suffering. Logotherapy and the Talmud operate from different dimensions, but there is a parallelism in their respective attitudes to suffering.

In addition, logotherapy maintains an openness to the religious dimension and does not hesitate to harness the patient's religiousness in effecting cure.

It would appear that the clinical framework of logotherapy is uniquely suited to properly coming to grips with problems of suffering among Jewish patients.

Chapter Eleven

LOGOTHERAPY AS A RESPONSE TO THE HOLOCAUST

No event, save the destruction of the Temple, has had such a shattering effect on Jewish life and thought as the holocaust. With the exception of atheists, who could use the holocaust as proof that there is no God, and the devouty religious, who could point to the holocaust as an indication that any salvation for the world is possible only through faith, the status quo has been demolished.

Responses to the holocaust have been varied, including a radical reformation of Judaism into a non-theology or paganism, as well as the reorientation of Judaism around a 614th commandment—never to let the holocaust recur and never to allow Jewish ranks to dissipate through cultural assimilation.

This essay proposes yet another response to the holocaust, a response with broad implications for the ultimate lesson mankind can learn from the human abyss reached in the Nazy tyranny.

II

The response is that of Dr. Viktor E. Frankl. Frankl's experiences in the four concentration camps he survived, and the human heights which he reached in that setting, are almost legendary.[1] The problem one faces in appreciating Frankl's courage is that his heroics seem almost super-human, a model of reaction reserved for a saint.[2] If, indeed, Frankl's is an almost transcendental reaction, it makes for good reading, and little more. Realistically, however, a response to this bestiality must be measured in terms of its pragmatic application, whether it affords the man in the street another possibility in his dialogue with life. Frankl affords this possibility, not in his personal story, rather in the philosophy of life which is projected in his logotherapy

Logotherapy, as some see it, is the third Viennese school of psychotherapy, overarching the Freudian and Adlerian schools. Logotherapy is an approach to life which asserts that the primary expression of the human person is to be seen in the striving to find a meaning in one's existence. Unlike his predecessors, who asserted the primariness of pleasure and power, respectively, Frankl insists on the importance of meaning for existentially viable life. Historically, Frankl's views predate the atrocities of the Second World War. Nevertheless, there is little doubt that the holocaust was the vital force which thrust logotherapy onto the intellectual scene, both as a psychological system and as a philosophy of life. The experiences of the concentration camps showed logotherapy to be more than grandiose preaching, and the pathos with which Frankl presented his case after the holocaust was the vital ingredient giving logotherapy a universal audience. World War II made the world more receptive to the deeply human cries of men like Frankl. That Frankl has translated his pathos into a system of life leads us to consider logotherapy as a response to the holocaust.

III

The most prevalent tone in all of Frankl's work is a basic and unshakeable optimism. Logotherapy begins with the notion that life possesses an objective, unconditional meaning in any and all circumstances, and in spite of all conditions, even suffering and death. The critical reader of Frankl is likely to be disenchanted by the overemphasis placed on the value of suffering and the meaning of death. Frankl, however, is less bothered by the meaning to be found in love or work, in health and pleasant conditions. Man's greatest problems are encountered in suffering and tragedy, and unconditional meaning can have validity only if this meaning can be inserted into the suffering situation. By giving meaning to suffering, Frankl is in effect saying that all life has meaning.

Frankl is a realist. Having lived through indescribable tortures and witnessing unbelievable cruelty, he is aware that most of man's life is spent not in the peaks of pleasure, but either in the nebulousness of spiritual mediocrity, or in the existential vacuum of meaninglessness. A sound approach to life must take into account these situations, else it would be geared to a precious few people, if not to a precious few moments. Logotherapy is for the man in the street, and Frankl pays prime attention to the man in the street in his empirical approach to life.

Logotherapy puts great emphasis on man's freedom. Man is able to meet any situation in the fullness of his human potential, and to react in the freedom of expression which is known as a human response. One of the ways man exhibits this freedom is in the stand he takes toward his fate, or his suffering. Man remains forever free to decide what his stand will be in spite of the most dismal circumstances. Undoubtedly the suffering situation might negate the possibility to be creative, but human values are possible also in the realm of attitudes. Attitude is the key, not only to the personal situation, but to logotherapy itself. The optimistic attitude Frankl takes to life dictates a meaning to suffering. Logotherapy tells man not just to endure suffering, but to find a meaning in it. Suffering, says Frankl, is what gives life its form and shape. Suffering is a part of life, and the right kind of suffering is the highest achievement that has been granted to man. In suffering, man transcends the physical situation into the noetic dimension, deciding in this self-detachment on the direction of his life. In the camps, Frankl repeatedly tried to convince the inmates their suffering had a meaning. If one had a book to write, or a loved one waiting for him, Frankl showed the meaning potential in survival. More important, even in the face of imminent doom, Frankl did not shrink from insisting on the meaningfulness of life. He would insist that every lived moment experienced by man remained in the world, even after death. To Frankl man's past cannot be erased from being but is instead the really meaningful aspect of being. How man has lived, how he has faced his suffering, can never be erased. His life is in the world, it remains in the world. Having been is the surest form of being. Man's past is his true future. This was Frankl in the concentration camps, and this is Frankl in the logotherapeutic clinic, trying to assuage the grief of a widow who has lost her husband after one year of marriage. What you experienced in that one year is and can never be taken away. And, because it is here forever, it forever remains a part of you.

Death, too, has meaning. Death is the final imprint man makes on his life—it is the monument of his life. Death rounds out life to its natural conclusion. It is the culmination of the becoming process. Frankl vehemently opposes euthanasia as it denies man the possibility to die his death. In death, man may transcend his self attitudinally, becoming, in that moment, an individual worthy of life. Compare "even if one is completely wicked all his life but repents at the end, he is not reproached with his wickedness."[3]

IV

In his attempts to elicit meaning out of potentially life-stopping situations, Frankl manifests an optimism which radiates throughout his logotherapy. Thus, suffering is not necessarily a tragic situation, for man can give meaning to his life by the way he meets his suffering. True, man can never fully know the real meaning of his suffering. He can only invest his suffering with meaning. Ultimately, the real meaning of suffering cannot be uncovered in a this-worldly dimension, but belongs, in Frankl's words, in the super-world, in the next higher dimension, or what theologians might call after-life. Man can never be sure of the meaning, but he is not asked to live in meaninglessness. He is asked to bear his incapacity to grasp the unconditional meaningfulness of the cosmos, of his own particular situation, as it is a super meaning. It is an optimistic orientation which underlines Frankl's repeated insistence on the meaningfulness of life. Logotherapy is not bothered by the state of unsureness about the particular meaning or the cosmological meaning. Man can, at one and the same time, be half sure and whole hearted, as Frankl is fond of quoting Allport. Perhaps one might add that in being sure, man is likely to be more mechanistic and less human, not striving and transcending as he is in search of the meaning.

Frankl's approach to death again points to his positive orientation, his affirmation of life. Without death, life would not be complete, he says. If man lived forever, he could constantly postpone the demands of the day with the argument there will always be a tomorrow. But the specter of death negates this argument, and the existential fact that any moment not used suffers its own existential death imposes an imperative for action on man in every moment of his existence.

The optimistic streak goes on. Man is guilty, but only in the face of guilt is it logical to talk of improving. Guilt implies a responsibleness for trespass, for if man is not responsible for the act he cannot be considered guilty. Responsibleness implies the free-willed decision of man, else he is not really responsible. That man is considered guilty is thus nothing less than an assertion he can erase the guilt.

Imperfection is a virtue in life. If man were perfect, if it were possible to be perfect, man's uniqueness would be destroyed, for there would be the common ground of perfection shared by man. The uniqueness of each individual inheres in the imperfections, and makes for the meaningfulness, the uniqueness and singularity of every existent being.

Man alone of all creatures retains the possibility of committing suicide. He alone can take his own life. Logotherapy transforms this into a positive feature of life. Since man can, at any time, terminate his life, his decision to remain alive is his way of saying "yes" to life. Since man is the only creature who can terminate his life, he is also the only creature who affirms life.

Why does boredom exist? Why is man plagued by the vacuity of having no task to perform? Logotherapy intervenes with its eternal optimism. If man did not feel the anguish of boredom, how could he become motivated to use all the time at his disposal usefully? Boredom is thus a necessity to motivate man into action.

Logotherapy, it may be said, turns life on its head. It refuses to capitulate to any situation except capitulation itself. In theory and therapy, it maintains that suffering gives meaning to life, that death can be a human act, that guilt is a positive force for man, that imperfection is a virtue for human endeavor, that the possibility of committing suicide is a uniquely human phenomenon, that boredom is a useful vacuum to elicit meaning. In short, logotherapy sees potential in every human fact and circumstance, meaning potential for man to actualize.

V

It remains for us to discover what logotherapy makes of the holocaust. Does the basic optimism which permeates logotherapy spill over into the holocaust, or is this the terminal point for optimism?

Because man can say "no" to life, he can also say "yes." More important, this yes is a meaningful human response. This point, extended a bit, reads as follows: Because man can be diabolically evil, he can also be virtuous. If man could do no evil, his good deeds would be no virtue. The price man pays for having been granted free choice is the potentiality for evil. Frankl repeatedly avers that he prefers a world in which such phenomena as Hitler are possible.[4] The possibilities for Hitlers are at the same time possibilities for saints. Such a world of choice is more preferable to a programmed world of conformism or collectivism, where man is forced to act as object of conditions, and his deeds are neither virtues nor vices.

Beyond the phenomenon of Hitler, Frankl makes clinical capital of the concentration camp experiences. The camps showed Freud to have miscalculated the human essence. Freud said that if any number of strongly differentiated human beings were subjected to equal amounts of starvation, the increasing desperation for food would blot out all individual differences, to be replaced by the uniform expression of the desire to feed the hunger. According to Frankl, the concentration camps proved Freud wrong. Scientifically the mind boggles at the thought of trying to establish a clinical situation in which Freud's thesis could be corroborated, yet the camps were, however unfortunately, a perfect setting to test Freud's hypothesis. In the camps, many people did degenerate into the innate camp bestiality, yet others transcended the conditions of the camp, exhibiting traits of saintliness that have become legend. There was not a uniform expression of the desire to satisfy hunger. Instead, there were men who sacrificed their own spoon of soup to help others get a foothold on life. The differences between the camp saint and the normal inmate resided in the realm of choice. Man is a deciding being, and the camps proved this fact of humanness once and for all. Man ultimately decides for himself.

Today, when Frankl is challenged to defend his notion of man's free will in the face of biological, sociological, and psychological determinants, he uses camp experience to defend his position. Man's destiny is shaped by his determining conditions, but nowhere has man been as constricted as in the camps. Still, man showed his capacity to brave and resist the worst conditions. For Frankl, the holocaust is empirical validation of man's freedom, and thus life's meaning.

Frankl faced the holocaust in great despair, yet his affirmative stance toward life did not allow despair to become resignation. Frankl did not question God. He saw the holocaust as the accident of man's free will, and, at the same time, as the testimony to man's powerful alternatives. Today, he continues to affirm life in his untiring preachments about the meaning of life. He sees his approach as a continuation of Akiba's affirmation of life "even if He (God) takes thy soul."[5] The holocaust transformed all his affirmative preachment into living reality, and Frankl's ability to find meaning in the holocaust reinforced his ability to endow all life with meaning.

VI

If we are to take inventory of the manifold responses to the destruction and havoc of the Nazi tyranny, and judge how they fit into Jewish thought, we will have to take more serious cognizance of Frankl's response.

And if we are ever able to judge whether anything positive has come out of the shambles of the crematoria, it is likely the life-affirmating system known as logotherapy will shine as a monument to the potential of man which was formed literally out of the dust and ashes of the gas ovens.

In a word, the credibility of logotherapy today is in large measure a result of the abyss which man experienced more than two decades ago. If logotherapy is successful in convincing man of his meaning potential, it will have resurrected from the past the human qualities that were slaughtered with the crudeness and mechanics of the beast. More than being a 614th commandment, it would become a rededication to life itself, and a reaffirmation of the positive potential in life.

SECTION 6

THE DAILY LIFESTYLE—LOVE AND LABOR

PRELUDE

The crisis in marriage today is perhaps best accentuated in the statistics which show over one-third of marriages ending in divorce and, if present trends continue, the rate could climb to one-half. Logotherapy has much to say about the meaning of love. *Chapter Twelve* presents these observations, the implementation of which would surely enhance the marriage picture.

The recent findings that 80% of the population feel they are in the wrong job for them, coupled with the unemployment figures, make the work situation a crucial topic of concern. *Chapter Thirteen* deals with the role of work in relation to the meaning of life. Again, the profound approach of logotherapy is a useful counter to distorted views prevalent in the work scene.

Love and labor are two classic illustrations of how concern for the ultimate enhances the immediate.

Chapter Twelve

THE MEANING OF LOVE

Logotherapy is the school of psychotherapy founded and nurtured by Viktor E. Frankl. It is commonly referred to as the third Viennese school of psychotherapy, following the schools of Freudian and Adlerian thought.

Logotherapy is, at once, an explicit philosophy and a clinical approach. In America, it is considered a humanistic psychology and is, as well, identified with the existential movement.

Logotherapy has much to say not only about the primary motivational force in individuals, but also focuses on the union of individuals, presenting theories on how such union is best effected and clinical approaches to enable the actualization of these theories.

An examination of logotherapy on marriage and the pertinence of its observations is the main topic of this chapter.

II

According to logotherapy, "the striving to find a meaning in one's life is the primary motivational force in man."[1] The meaning potential indigenous to humans resides in the spiritual dimension. Humans are primarily spiritual beings, with the term "spiritual" signifying that which makes individuals human rather than implying any theological posture. The spiritual dimension is the overarching dimension, embracing the other dimensions such as the instinctual, and potentially even raising instinct, through the proper attitude, to the spiritual level.

Logotherapy posits three fundamental philosophical notions which are the cornerstone of its system. They are: (1) freedom of will, (2) will to meaning, and (3) meaning of life.[2] The notion of *freedom of will* asserts that individuals are at all times free to search for and find meaning. Instinct, heredity, and environmental factors are seen as elements shaping destiny but not dictating it. "People may have instincts, but the instincts do not have them." In fact, freedom is contingent upon destiny. The host of restrictions surrounding the individual serve as the parameters within which choice is conceivable. "Man is not free from conditions but is and always remains free to take a stand toward whatever conditions he may have to face," says Frankl. The absence of a destiny circumscribed by physical and environmental factors would make freedom an impossibility. Within the confines of destiny, the critical ingredient is the attitude taken to a specific trait. It is in human hands to decide whether the lust to spill blood translates into murder or surgery, whether cunning becomes thievery or the practive of law. Man ultimately decides for himself.

The *will to meaning* is the mediating principle between subject and object, between the individual and the value-world. In freedom, the individual wills toward finding a meaning, rather than being driven toward it. To reduce the search for meaning to an urge or drive is to make meaning the tool through which to release tension and achieve homeostasis. Such meaning would then be meaningless, and a biological rather than human expression. Humans are not primarily concerned with pleasure or power. Pleasure pursued is pleasure eluded. In Frankl's view, pleasure cannot be a goal, it is rather the by-product of a meaningful life, and, as Frankl see it, power also is not an end in itself, but rather the means toward the finding of meaning. People who lust for power are usually denied it or are destroyed in their attaining it. Primarily, the healthy human expression inheres in willing to find and actualize a meaning.

Meaning of life, the third of these interrelated principles, posits the notion of the unconditional meaningfulness of life in any and all circumstances. Meaning is realized through values lived, be they the creative values of giving to the world, experiential values of taking in from the world, or attitudinal values in terms of the stance taken toward an unchangeable fate or situation. Meaning is objective. If meaning were subjective, it would be dependent on subjective feelings, and thus compromise meaning's unconditionality. As objective, the meaning is outside the individual, and demands the process of self-transcendence to be fulfilled. In Frankl's view, the person's humanness is realized in "self-transcendence" and not in self-expression. Self-expression and the desire for self-realization are self-defeating as goals and can only ensue as the tangential benefits of proper meaning orientation.

A healthy tension exists between the subjective "I am" and the objective "I ought." The interplay in this dynamic process of bridging the is-ought gap is the key to the human model.

To be sure, logotherapy is a profound approach to life. Frankl has laid it down in twenty-three books, of which so far only six are available in English. These few paragraphs distill the vastness of his teachings into basic fundamentals in order to make an excursion into logotherapy on marriage more intelligible.

III

Love is a vital component of human expression. As a human expression, true love penetrates into the innermost core of the individual, the spiritual essence.

> Loving (in the narrowest sense of the word) represents the end state of eroticism (in the broadest sense of the word), since it alone penetrates as deeply as possible into the personal structure of the partner. Loving represents a coming to relationship with another as a spiritual being. The close connection with spiritual aspects of the partner is the ultimate attainable form of partnership.[3]

The truly human love, as the truly human life, exists in the spiritual dimension, and is a "spiritual" relationship between individuals.

Logotherapy emphasizes the responsibleness of the individual to life, the person's being responsible for the fulfillment of meaning. This responsibleness is based on each person's uniqueness and singularity. Uniqueness is a spiritual attribute, for both physical and psychic traits may be duplicated. In the spiritual dimension, each individual is unique, with an essence different from any other being. "Uniqueness is what constitutes man's personhood," says Frankl. At the same time, the existence of each unique being is *singular,* in that each moment can only be lived once and can never be retrieved. The imperative to act flows from the responsibleness rooted in the unique individual capacities combined with the singularity of each moment. It is a responsibleness not to waste the self or time For, in Frankl's own words, "each moment is irrepeatable, and each person irreplaceable."

Uniqueness and singularity are also determinants in Frankl's concept of love:

> Love is living the experience of another person in all his uniqueness and singularity. . . . In love the beloved person is comprehended in his very essence, as the unique and singular being that he is; he is comprehended as a Thou, and as such is taken into the self.[4]

Universal love is recognition and appreciation of the uniqueness and singularity of the world's inhabitants. Personal love is living the experience of one individual, acknowledging that person's otherness and infinite potential, and effecting its evolution. Here, Frankl admittedly leans heavily on the great German phenomenologist Max Scheler.

Uniqueness implies the realization that the partner is irreplaceable. In true love the partners are not concerned with what the other "has"; instead they focus on what the other "is." What each one "is" is unique, and cannot be duplicated. The concept of singularity espouses the value of each moment in the love relationship, and, if properly understood, serves as a guarantee never to neglect or take the other for granted.

Frankl believes that love is undeserved:

> As a human person he becomes for the one who loves him indispensable and irreplaceable without having done anything to bring this about. The person who is loved "can't help" having the uniqueness and singularity of his self—that is, the value of his personality—realized. Love is not deserved, is unmerited—it is simply grace.[5]

If love could be defined concretely, that is, as something partners have either separately or together, it would then follow that this concrete entity called love is caused by what each partner has. Love would be deserved through the concrete causal qualities possessed by each partner. Instead, love is something that simply "is." Immersion in the personality of the other is a manifestation of this undefinable. Living the uniqueness and singularity of the other is the overriding feature of true love. It is how love asserts itself, but is not what love really is. Love is a quality, an infinite quality, and, like life, defies reductionistic definitions.

IV

Frankl calls love "the ultimate and the highest goal to which man can aspire."[6] True love as immersion in the other presupposes the capacity of the individual for self-transcendence. In self-transcendence, the person is able to concentrate on values and beings that are outside the self, instead of yearning for self-realization or self-expression. In order to love, one must transcend the self toward another being or cause.

> Man is never concerned primarily with himself but, by virtue of his self-transcendent quality, he endeavors to serve a cause higher than himself, or to love another person. Loving and serving a cause are the principal manifestations of this self-transcendent quality of human existence that has been totally neglected by closed-system concepts such as the homeostasis principle.[7]

Love facilitates the mutual self-transcendence of both partners. Love opens up a new world of values and gives to the partners a heightened receptivity to these values.

The objective world of values is brought into sharper focus and the actualization of these infinite values is thus facilitated. In this process the personalities of the lovers themselves are developed. "In the mutual surrender of love, in the giving and taking between two people, each one's own personality comes into its own."[8]

Self-fulfillment is a self-defeating process when inner oriented. Self-fulfillment is the automatic outgrowth of an orientation towards transcendence. Love contains its greatest meaning in this context, for it opens up the world of possibility and effects its actualization. Frankl believes that by making the beloved person aware of the inherent potential, the lover helps the beloved make these potentialities into actualities.

There is a dialectical process at work. The loved one wants to be worthy of the lover, and grow more and more like the lover's image. Each one, in a manner of speaking, outbids the other to be worthier and thus elevates the other. Frankl here enunciates in philosophical terms the wisdom of the world, which characterizes a good relationship with the phrase "they bring out the best in each other," and a bad relationship through the phrase "they bring out the worst in each other."

In love, there is an upward spiral which causes both partners to attain heights otherwise unreachable. Love is thus the existential accelerator and actualizer of the individual's fulfillment.

Frankl takes pains to emphasize that although love can give meaning to life, a life without love is not meaningless. Meaning is unconditional, and love an effective means to meaning, but there are other avenues to meaning fulfillment. Meaning is realized not merely through what is given or denied, rather through the attitude and approach taken. An unhappy love experience can start a process of self-investigation leading to true fulfillment. Meaning is never in anticipation; it is recognized retroactively through the quality one gives to each situation.

V

Frankl's theory on the role of sex in the love relationship follows from his contention concerning the pursuit of pleasure. He says that:

> Actually, man does not care for pleasure and happiness as such but rather for that which causes these effects, be it the fulfillment of a personal meaning, or the encounter with a human being.[9]

For the healthy person, pleasure and happiness are side benefits of meaning fulfillment. If sex is considered the pleasure aspect of the love relationship, then one's primary concern is the love itself, the spiritual core of the other. The body expresses the character, and the character expresses the person as a spiritual being. The spirit demands and attains expression in the body. The bodily appearance is a symbol of what the beloved really is. Arousal is stimulated by the body, but the love itself is not directed toward the body; instead, it is directed to the other's being.

In true love, sex is not an end in itself but follows naturally from the essence of the relationship.

> But for the real lover the physical, sexual relationship remains a mode of expression for the spiritual relationship which his love really is, and as a mode of expression it is love, the spiritual act, which gives it human dignity.[10]

The sexual act is the symbolic immersion in the totality of the partner, and opens up an ultimate togetherness.

For Frankl, sex is really human sex only when it is the expression of love. Love is not seen as an epiphenomenon of sexual drives. Instead, love is a primary phenomenon. Sex is justified and sanctified only as long as it is a vehicle of love. It is not sex which brings love, rather it is the love which has, as its unique language, sex.

Were sex anything less than expression of a deeply rooted relationship, the partner would be reduced to a mechanistic source for the satiation of a sexual appetite. The partner would become a mutual means toward an end, and all physical communication a desecration of individual dignity.

Within this framework, a love relationship does not disintegrate when sex is impossible. If the love is primary, and sex a mere expression of that love, then, in situations where renunciation is called for, the love will remain unabated.

VI

Marriage does not follow necessarily from the presence of love, even true love in the spiritual sense. Marriage demands the satisfactions of certain societal conditions basic to a functioning union. At times, the dictates of love argue strongly in favor of desisting from marriage: if, for example, the other conditions necessary for a viable togetherness are missing, thus almost guaranteeing failure.

At the same time, love is the most important precondition for marriage. Marriage becomes a possibility only when true love exists.

The marriage bond is by its very nature exclusive. Frankl, as previously mentioned, indicates that love is manifested in the experiencing of the other in the other's uniqueness and singularity. Singularity is the implicit imperative to realize the value of each moment and actualize it. In marriage, it is the imperative to the spouses to transcend their selves together and ascend the infinite heights of objective values. Any action by either spouse which suspends this vertical movement is, in a wider context, a form of infidelity. Infidelity need not be consigned to the ultimate, another affair, but refers to any endeavor which might stagnate or obstruct the couple's striving to attain a meaningful co-existence. An exclusive, or monogamous, union is just one of the external conditions which must be satisfied for marriage to prosper.

If love is the recognition by each parner of the unique potentialities of the other, then marriage is the agreement by both to mutually meet the world of values as a committed whole, and to complement each other in the actualizing of these values. A partner trespasses the agreement of matrimony when indulging in any diversionary act which neglects or negates the other. Since marriage is commitment to infinite possibility, there is no moment in the union which does not afford the opportunity to realize values, or fulfill the potential meaning of two lives spent together.

Willful disregard of the singularity of the union manifests itself in many forms, each destroying the exclusiveness of the bond. In this respect, the individual must be guilty, in marriage, of the same deviances that abound in the everyday confrontation with life, namely, the failure to realize all possible values. The finiteness of the individual combined with the infinite possibility of life dictates this guilt. Awareness of this is-ought gap is a healthy state of being, for it at once acknowledges what might have been and what can still become.

In a true love relationship, fidelity in its wider sense is automatic and jealousy impossible. As Frankl has pointed out, either true love exists, in which case jealousy is impossible, or the relationship is not one of true love, in which case there is nothing to be jealous about.

The dynamics of fidelity in the framework of logotherapy work in a specific direction. "Certainly fidelity is one of love's tasks; but it is always a task only for the lover and can never be a demand directed at the partner."[11] Logotherapy sees life itself as a task, with the individual being confronted by life. It is not for the person to make demands on life; instead, the individual must respond to it. "Don't ask what you may have to expect from life," recommended Frankl, in his book on his concentration camp experiences (published in German as early as in 1946), "but ask what life expects from you." In love, the same process is at work. Faithfulness cannot be demanded, it must ensue as the mirror reflection of each partner's commitment.

This ideal of love and marriage is not the norm, even though it is philosophically sound and clinically justified. For many, marriage involves union with a type, easily found and easily replaceable.

> Today's average man takes this type of woman for his erotic ideal because she cannot, in her impersonality, burden him with responsibility. The type is ubiquitous. Just as one chorus-girl in the revue can be replaced by any other, so in life this type of woman is easily replaceable. The chorus-girl type is impersonal woman with whom a man need have no personal relationship, no obligations; a woman he can "have" and therefore need not love. She is property, without personal traits, without personal value.[12]

The very nature of such a relationship invites its breakdown, for infidelity follows from impersonality. Frankl has also pointed out that where the quality of love is missing, it is compensated by quantity of sexual pleasure.

VII

Logotherapy's theory of life and love appears to be highly moralistic and idealistic, almost unattainable for mere mortals. It should be pointed out that what appears as moral preachment is really empirical wisdom, the wisdom of the heart, retranslated from its phenomenological context into the language of the man in the street.[13] It may seem to be beyond the reach of ordinary people, but one should not desist from making proposals. In fact, Frankl calls his idealism "the real realism."[14] *Humane* humans are, and will probably always remain, a minority. "It is precisely for this reason that each of us is challenged to *join* the minority."[15]

Logotherapy is rooted in an examination of what is necessary for humans to achieve a state of health. The search for meaning is the primary motivational force not because moral law so dictates, but because the human being is best off when oriented in the meaning direction. The authentic striving for meaning eventuates in pleasure and self-fulfillment automatically and pushes away the possibility of existential frustration or "noogenic neurosis." The ideal human is a healthy spiritual being, and logotherapy derives from the ideal. Therapy often involves bridging the gap between the real and the ideal, or changing the static thinking of the patient to an outward, future-oriented frame of mind.

Marriage itself offers a clear illustration of how the failure of an ideal leads to the breakdown of the real.

The true love relationship cannot be grounded in the striving for self-fulfillment, or even in the mere fulfillment of the other;

> we must recognize that this dialogue defeats itself unless I and thou transcend themselves to refer to a meaning outside themselves.[16]

Just as the individual is fulfilled tangentially through the actualization of values, so the dual individuality which is the married couple fulfill their selves through that which is outside them, the objective world of meanings and values.

In this ideal relationship, sex is the language of love, as natural and automatic as speech. But, as to happiness deriving from sex, Frankl cautions, again and again, that "happiness cannot be pursued, it must ensue."

> The more a male client tries to demonstrate his potency, the more he is likely to become impotent, and the more a female client tries to demonstrate to herself that she is capable of fully experiencing orgasm, the more liable she is to be caught in frigidity.[17]

The approach of logotherapy in cases of sexual dysfunction is to put the matter of sex into proper perspective.

> A young woman came to me complaining of being frigid. The case history showed that in her childhood she had been sexually abused by her father. However, it was not this traumatic experience in itself that had eventuated in her sexual neurosis, as could easily be evidenced. For it turned out that, through reading popular psychoanalytic literature, the patient had lived all the time in the fearful expectation of the toll that her traumatic experience would some day take. This anticipatory anxiety resulted in both excessive intention to confirm her femininity and excessive attention centered upon herself rather than upon her partner. This was enough to incapacitate the patient for the peak experience of sexual pleasure, since the orgasm is made an object of intention and an object of attention as well, instead of remaining an unintended effect of unreflected commitment to the partner. After undergoing short-term logotherapy, the patient's excessive attention and intention of her ability to experience orgasm was "de-reflected," to introduce another logotherapeutic term. When her attention was refocused toward the proper object, i.e., the partner, orgasm established itself spontaneously.[18]

The logotherapist is likely to use "de-reflection" and proper intention to counter sexual dysfunction. Another logotherapeutic improvisation might be to permit the sexually problemed patient every access to the spouse except the sexual act itself, for "medical" reasons. The person is now de-reflected from sex, has forgotten about it, and is surely not intending it. The logotherapist will feign amazement when shortly thereafter, as is likely, the patient will apologetically admit that the doctor's orders were not needed, that the sexual act flowed naturally and could not be stopped. Sahakian and Sahakian[19] suggest that in the technique of de-reflection

The Meaning of Love

Frankl anticipated by many years—in fact, in 1947—the sex therapy approach of Masters and Johnson.

What is true of sexual dysfunction in the narrow sense is true of marital dysfunction in the wider sense. Weiss, in exploring the reasons for the high divorce rate in America, says that

> To a greater extent than seems true elsewhere in the world, we Americans seem to cherish our right to the unimpeded pursuit of happiness, no matter how much sorrow that pursuit may engender.[20]

Beyond this, there is a heavy accent on the realization of the inner potential for growth, development, and expression, what could be termed the "ethic of self-realization." It seems that more and more some aspect of this ethical position is given as a reason for impatience with marriage. And,

> In several instances in which the pursuit of self-realization did not itself produce the separation, it seemed nevertheless to have contributed to marital strife.[21]

Is it possible that the high rate of divorce can be traced back to a philosophy? And, from a clinical view, is it possible that marital problems can be cured through a re-orientation toward a different philosophy?

Allport once asked:

> May not (sometimes at least) an acquired world-outlook constitute the central motive of a life, and, if it is disordered, the ultimate therapeutic problem?[22]

Given Allport's approach and Weiss's views regarding the increase in marital breakdown, it would appear that many cases of marriage difficulty are rooted in a disordered philosophy. Logotherapy's philosophy of self-transcendence as opposed to the "ethic of self-realization" seems as logical a curative for the disordered marriage as its technique of dereflection is a curative for disordered sex.

Chapter Thirteen
THE WORK SITUATION: LOGOTHERAPEUTIC AND TALMUDIC PERSPECTIVES

One characteristic feature of the search for identity in Western society is the tendency to equate one's job with the purpose of one's life. This is reflected in the problems which arise from unhappiness at work, the syndrome of malaise which is directly linked to lack of employment, and the stress on career which is heavily accented in the women's movement, to cite but a few examples.

Modern society needs a philosophy of work which is sensitive not only to human needs, but also to ultimate human concerns. This philosophy of work must relate to the clinical and meta-clinical implications of employment and unemployment.

Viktor Frankl's logotherapy, which, aside from projecting the notion of meaning into prominence, also coined the term "unemployment neurosis" to describe the negative effects of joblessness, seems uniquely suited to respond to this need for a philosophy of work.

According to Frankl, "Life is a task."[1] Something or Someone outside the individual confronts the person, eliciting the performance of certain tasks One must dedicate the self to this call.

> Man's struggle for his self and his identity is doomed to failure unless it is enacted as dedication and devotion to something beyond his self, to something above his self.[2]

One is constantly faced by the objective value world, and through the subject-object tension is called upon to transcend the self toward translating the values out there in the world into reality. The task in life is a never-ending process. "We must never be content with what has already been achieved.

Life never ceases to put new questions to us, never permits us to come to rest."[3]

This is reminiscent of the Talmudic dictum "it is not incumbent upon you to finish the work, but neither are you free to desist from it."[4]

The response to life's challenge, in Frankl's view, is in activity. Since the meaning of life is unconditional, not to be questioned but to be responded to, "it follows from this that the response should be given not in words, but in acting, by doing."[5]

No two responses are alike. The uniqueness of each person and the singularity of each situation indicate the particular nature of the response. The approach to one's mission in life may be interpreted as the dynamic of one's seeking "to find his way to his own proper task, to advance toward the uniqueness and singularity of his own meaning in life."[6]

The understanding of one's uniqueness and singularity, or, one's responsibility to life, is a retrospective process. One desires to derive what ought to be from what is, but the best way to find out who we are is not through reflecting on the question, but through action. Frankl goes on to quote Goethe's dictum. "Try to do your duty and you will soon find out what you are. But what is your duty? The demands of each day."[7]

The person is thus involved in a trial and error process in seeking one's proper place in the cosmos. In any direction the individual turns, there must be preparedness for the posssibility that the approach taken is not the correct one. This demands flexibility on the part of the individual to recognize which approach is conducive to the actualization of values in the context of potential choices. "Life requires of man spiritual elasticity, so that he may temper his efforts to the chances that are offered."[8]

The ultimate justification of each person's existence depends less on whether one reaches the goal and more on the intensity with which one strives to reach it.

> That he must aim at the best is imperative; otherwise his efforts would come to nought. But at the same time he must be able to content himself with nothing more than approaching nearer and nearer, without ever quite attaining his goal.[8]

Or, as Frankl expresses it, "Things are bad. But unless we do our best to improve them, everything will become worse."[10]

A Talmudic counterpart of this notion is found in the statement that "one may acquire eternity in a single hour another may acquire it after many years."[11] Though this Talmudic statement differs in some respects, it nevertheless speaks about the unknowability of one's real purpose, and implies the importance of striving to fulfill one's purpose.

Orientation around one's task in life, the perpetual approach to the infinite value world, is crucial to the individual's well-being. "There is nothing in the world, I dare say, which helps man so efficiently to survive and keep healthy as the knowledge of a life task."[12] Frankl indicates that this conscious awareness of having a task in life was a positive force in the Nazi concentration camps. Those who were aware of a task awaiting them were the most likely to survive. Orientation around a task is thus seen to have meta-clinical value. Moreover, it is seen as that which is most likely to help the individual overcome difficulty.

There is an added dimension to the concept of task which emanates from the perception that the specific task is specially directed to the self. This makes of the task a mission. "Having such a task makes the person irreplaceable and gives his life the value of uniqueness."[13]

II

Work, or the individual's calling, should not be confused with the individual's life task. What one works at is not necessarily what one is or the vehicle toward becoming what one ought to be. "There is a false identification of one's calling with the life task to which one is called."[14] One may achieve the life task through work, but not necessarily through work. Frankl conceives of work in a sociological context.

> Work usually represents the area in which the individual's uniqueness stands in relation to society and thus acquires meaning and value. This meaning and value, however, is attached to the person's work as a contribution to society, not to the actual occupation as such.[15]

This, in fact, is Frankl's conception of what society means by work. In Frankl's philosophy meaning must be elicited from all life experience, work included. One is called upon to choose a calling which will contain meaning and to reject a perhaps more financially rewarding calling which does not offer the same opportunity for meaning fulfillment. The criteria for choosing work, in Frankl's view, contain a sociological factor, but must contain other factors which do not reduce the person to being merely a source of production.

Frankl exemplifies this point with the illustration of a young person who transcended poverty circumstances and became a physician. He was offered a lucrative post which, however, did not relate to his special talent. The choice was between being successful or having inner fulfillment. Were this man to dedicate himself to his specialty, he would, through his vocation, find meaning in his life. The critical factor is the human ingredient in the choice.[16]

The human ingredient is also crucial in the actual work. Frankl stresses the importance of what one gives to one's position rather than what one takes from it, a distinct departure from the consumer ethic. "A humble country doctor who is firmly rooted in his locality may seem a greater man than many of his successful metropolitan colleagues."[17]

Even given similar outward circumstances, as in the case of two people with the same calling, one may translate the role into a meaningful endeavor while the other may see it as a rote exercise and do the job listlessly.

> The meaning of the doctor's work lies in what he does beyond his purely medical duties; it is what he brings to his work as a personality, as a human being, which gives the doctor his peculiar role. For it would come to the same thing whether he or a colleague gave injections, etc., if he were merely practicing the arts of medicine, merely using the tricks of the trade. Only when he goes beyond the limits of purely professional service, beyond the tricks of the trade, does he begin that truly personal work which alone is fulfilling.[18]

Generally, work can be meaningful if it is raised above the level of rote behavior into the human sphere, if the individual essence is injected into the calling. It matters little what the nature of the job is; what counts is what the individual brings to the job that is unique and irreplaceable.

Frankl recognizes that work may sometimes retard the person's search for meaning. He cites the case of a diplomat who had been undergoing psychoanalysis for a number of years because he was unhappy in his position. He came to Frankl to continue treatment. Frankl relates:

> After a few interviews, it was clear that his will to meaning was frustrated by his vocation, and he actually longed to be engaged in some other kind of work. As there was no reason for not giving up his profession and embarking on a different one, he did so, with most gratifying results.[19]

Job-hopping is not an unknown occurrence in contemporary society, often in situations which appear as retrograde switches. The myth of fulfillment in high position, as evidenced in the case of the diplomat, is based on the erroneous identification of high position with contentment or meaningfulness. Position itself cannot bring the meaning. Meaning evolves from the effective dialectic between the person and the job. Where that dialectic is missing, it is best to explode the myth and change jobs.

There are also occupations which by their very nature may be considered meaningless exercises. In such instances, one is forced into a different approach, gearing the preoccupation with meaning fulfillment to the after work hours.

The boring daily routine of performing repetitive tasks, of putting in the same parts in the assembly line, more than likely excludes meaning from its domain.

> In such circumstances, it is true, work can be conceived only as a mere means to an end, the end of earning money—that is, earning the necessary means for real life. In this case real life begins only with the person's leisure time, and the meaning of that life consists in giving form to that leisure.[20]

Frankl insists there is no situation in life which is meaningless. The meaning of life is unconditional, i.e., available under any circumstances, and in this sense, independent of circumstances.

Material gains from one's vocation are important for meaning fulfillment. They are "generally a prerequisite for meaning fulfillment."[21] However, Frankl cautions against making the means an end in itself, as such an attitude divests life of a proper direction. The "will to meaning" then may degenerate into a mere "will to money," he observes.

Frankl tells the story of an American University president who offered him $9,000 to serve on the University faculty for a few weeks. Frankl refused. The president naturally thought Frankl wanted more money. Frankl assured him this was not the case. Rather, he said,

> If I pondered how to invest the nine thousand dollars I should say that there is one worthwhile way in which to invest it, and that is to buy time for work. But I now have time for work, so why should I sell it for nine thousand dollars?[22]

III

The person can live a meaningful life even without an occupation, as the meaning of life is unconditional. However, Frankl admits, it is understandable that an unemployed person should feel a vacuum within. Having no occupation, the person feels useless and sees life as devoid of meaning. This is bound to lead to what Frankl terms "unemployment neurosis."

> Just as idle organs in the body may become the hosts for rampant growths, so idleness in the psychological realm leads to morbid inner development. Unemploymen becomes a culture medium for proliferation of neuroses.[23]

The Talmud recognized this possible consequence of worklessness when it asserted that "idleness leads to idiocy."[24]

The retired person is also prone to the vacuum created by lack of employment, or to what Frankl calls "retirement neurosis." Even the person with gainful employment is not exempt from the effects of unemployment, suffering sometimes from what Frankl has branded "Sunday neurosis." This is a depression which plagues those who suddenly become aware of the void in their lives when the pressure of work abates momentarily.

These are instances where a bad philosophy translates into what may become a clinical problem.

> What actually reduces the neurotic unemployed to apathy, what ultimately underlies the unemployment neurosis, is the erroneous view that working is the only meaning of life. There is a false identification of one's calling with the life task to which one is called. This incorrect equating of the two necessarily makes the unemployed person suffer from the sense of being useless and superfluous.[25]

Frankl sees the role of logotherapy as vital to the elimination of the vacuum created by unemployment. The individual must be made aware that the attitude of hopelessness is unwarranted and that, in spite of all, life still affords the chance to live meaningfully. The logotherapist in encountering people suffering from a sense of meaninglessness does not impose values or give direction to a specific form of meaning, but rather opens up the value world, setting into motion the wheels of discovery. The rest is up to the patient. The patient must decide how to transcend the immediate predicament, to stop despairing and instead start to focus on the meaning possibilities which exist.

IV

There is a further aspect to the work situation which Frankl addresses. It concerns the notion of work in the religious dimension. There are people who also experience the authority from which the task comes.

> In our opinion, we have here an essential characteristic of the religious man: he is a man who interprets his existence not only in terms of being responsible *for* fulfilling his life tasks, but also as being responsible *to* the taskmaster.[26]

The Talmud, which sees work in this religious dimension, focuses on aspects of work in a manner which Frankl parallels, although Frankl himself confines his professional writings deliberately to the secular framework.

The Talmud sees toil as part of spiritual growth. "The Divine presence rests upon the individual neither through gloom, nor through sloth."[27] The Talmud thus establishes a correlation between work and meaning, a correlation which is intended to preclude laziness from the human endeavor. In this context, the work referred to by the Talmud is closer to the notion of task than to the notion of job.

The Talmud explains the statement "every person is born for toil" as referring to toiling in the Torah.[28] The approach to meaning (Torah) is thus directly linked with the approach to labor. In a world where everything is prepared, a paradise of sorts, the individual would naturally sink into laxity. With no challenge to physical well-being, as sustenance is guaranteed, one would not feel compelled to work. The structure of the world is such that one is confronted every day with hunger and possible starvation. In this framework, one is forced to labor for bread.

Recognizing that physical existence is contingent on labor, the individual should then carry the work factor to its natural conclusion. Not only the physical self, but also the spiritual essence demand proper toil to effect fulfillment. In letting things happen too naturally, one starves the self spiritually as well as physically. One must labor on the self to elicit meaning from life and ensure existence of its ultimate worth.

This may seem like preachment, almost as much as Frankl's philosophy sometimes seems like preachment. In fact, they are not preachments as much as they are reflections on what brings out the best in the person in clinical and metaclinical realms.

Confrontation with life's responsibilities is established by the Talmud as an Employer-employee relationship, with God the Employer and the human being the employee—in fact, a work metaphor. "Know before whom you toil, and who is your Employer who will pay you the reward of your labor"[29] states the essence of life's confrontation. Through work one understands the full import of human existence. Work becomes the entity in life which brings to reality the relationship of the person to the Creator, and is thus a basic necessity for the human situation.

If the confrontation relationship is that of employer to employee, then one's existence in life is a task, or metaphysical work. "The day is short and the work is much"[30] projects the infinite aspect of this task. The day, one's sojourn on earth, is finite, whilst the work, the actualization of values, is limitless, reminiscent of the never-completed subject-object dynamic in logotherapy.

Work, and the likely aquisition of wealth, are seen by the Talmud as the means to fulfillment, not as ends in themselves. "The more property, the more anxiety"[31] expresses the Talmudic view that the striving for wealth creates problems which divert the person from meaning orientation, akin to the directionlessness alluded to by Frankl.

According to the Talmud, "One's money should always be ready to hand,"[32] an observation which relates to the meaning of wealth. The money is entrusted to the person as the means through which to help others, and to thus find meaning through living the values of sharing and concern. "If a dollar can serve more meaning and purpose in the hands of anyone else I must not keep it in my own pocket book,"[33] says Frankl.

Even when the meaning associated with wealth is not a realistic possibility, the avenues of meaning and purpose are not closed off. "No one is poor save one who lacks knowledge."[34] This applies equally to one who despairs of life for lack of wealth and to one who rejects the essence of life in the pursuit of means rather than meaning.

In effect, one must be able to divorce circumstance from purpose.

> Such is the way of the Torah: A morsel of bread with salt you shall eat, and water by measure you shall drink, and upon the ground you shall sleep, and a life of privation you shall live, and in the Torah you shall labor.[35]

The Talmud is not hereby recommending the ascetic approach to life, as this is inconsistent with basic Talmudic thought. Instead, the idea projected here is that the person should be able, theoretically, and, if necessary by circumstance (poverty or unemployment), to conceive of meaning (Torah) in any situation, however difficult. It is an unconditionality which is not unlike that proposed by Frankl in his meaning philosophy.

Whether it is in plenty or in poverty, in work or in unemployment, the key is the attitude to the situation. "Let all your actions be for the sake of the name of Heaven"[36] is the theological counterpart of the logotherapeutic insistence on approaching all life conditions within the meaning perspective.

It would appear that just as the philosophy-psychology of work proposed by Frankl is a welcome corrective in this age of job-turbulence, so is the Talmud's parallel but dimensionally different theology-philosophy-psychology uniquely equipped to deal with the work dilemma in the religious dimension. Both may be employed as existential preventives and clinical cures.

SECTION 7

TIMELESS TRUTH

PRELUDE

The final chapter, *Chapter Fourteen,* is anecdotal in nature. It compares logotherapy and hasidic wisdom on the themes of free will, the nature of human striving, value orientation, the element of meaning, attitudes to despair, suffering and death, the nature of love, and perspectives on work and material gain.

The similarities between logotherapy and Hasidism, in spite of the fact that they work from different dimensions, are striking. The greatest common factor is the love of people and appreciation of their potential. This is the root from which the attitude to various life situations emanates.

The commonality of the two systems is vivid illustration that the verities espoused by logotherapy are not fads or instant reactions, rather they are timeless truths.

Chapter Fourteen

HASIDISM AND LOGOTHERAPY:

ENCOUNTER THROUGH ANTHOLOGY

In the experience of Viktor Frankl, architect of logotherapy, reactions to his lectures seem to vary with the place where the lecture is given. Generally, when Frankl travels east, what he says is not greeted with as much enthusiasm as when he speaks in the western world. The eastern world seems to think of logotherapy as something which they knew all along. In the west, logotherapy seems to be something novel.

Frankl has never claimed that his system is, in fact, something new under the sun. He takes the approach that one must rediscover the basic truths of human existence. Logotherapy, in fact, is geared towards facilitating this discovery. It, therefore, would seem quite pertinent to illustrate the similarity logotherapy shares with eastern tradition by comparing logotherapy with some basic notions of Hasidism, the movement launched by Rabbi Israel Baal Shem Tov in the middle of the 18th century. In fact, Hasidism is rooted in Jewish mystical tradition and has branched forth with many different "schools" headed by leaders called *Rebbes* and peopled with varying numbers of disciples.

Instead of taking any specific doctrine, this presentation focuses on incidents and statements associated with many of the hasidic rabbis and offers a logotherapeutic counterpart to each incident or observation.

The hasidic incidents referred are mainly those which be found in *The Hasidic Anthology*.[1] This is used as it contains a broad base of subject topics which incorporate the ideas of many of the hasidic masters and is also an easily accessible volume.

The logotherapeutic counterparts herein projected are mainly not direct quotes of Frankl but rather the paraphrasing of ideas either directly expressed by Frankl or graphically implied in the system Frankl develops.

II

This section deals with the notion of free-will in Hasidism and logotherapy.

Hasidism—The Koretzer Rebbe reflected on the fact that if one's desires are weakened as the body declines, what happens to free will? Contrary to the argument that such an individual might sin less because there is a weaker impulse to sin, the Koretzer maintained that the impulse, though it may be weaker because the body is weakening, is nevertheless strong by force of habit. Besides, the power of resistance is commensurately weakened.

Logotherapy—The individual in all situations and all circumstances always retains the free will to take a stand toward those circumstances.

Hasidism—According to Rabbi Israel Baal Shem Tov, one should learn pride but not be proud, one should learn anger but not feel angry, for the person should be complete, possessing all human traits.

The Koretzer observed that one cannot be consciously good unless one knows evil. One cannot appreciate pleasure unless one has experienced bitterness. Good is merely the opposite of evil, as is pleasure the opposite of anxiety. Without the evil impulse one could do no evil but neither could one do good.

Logotherapy—It is preferable to have a world in which even Hitler is possible rather than one in which all individuals are programmed. Such programming destroys the element of choice and makes of any good behavior an action devoid of the human ingredient and therefore, lacking meaning. It is only because of the possibility of evil that choice is possible.

Hasidism—The Dzikover Rebbe stopped an individual and asked what he would do if he found a purse of money. The fellow replied instantly—I would return it to the owner, of course. The rabbi said he had too quick an answer and that it was probably insincere. Another one responded that he would probably keep it if he could. The rabbi said that he was wicked. The Dzikover then approached an unlearned hasid who responded—Rabbi, it would be such a great temptation. I would beg God to give me the strength to withstand it and thus enable me to perform the commandment of returning a lost article. The rabbi acknowledged that this answer was proper and correct. He further said that it was proper for a hasid to give such an answer. Opponents of Hasidism blame us for accepting unlearned persons as Hasidim, he said, but this shows the influence of hasidic instruction even among the unlearned.

Logotherapy—It is quite useful to learn from the wisdom of the man in the street. Sometimes there is a tension in human action which involves doing what one ought to do as opposed to what one would like to do. It might be pertinent here to relate a story told by Frankl[2] of a Jewish army doctor who, during World War I, hid in the ditches together with his dear friend, a high-ranking aristocrat who was also a colonel, while the heavy bombing of the Italian/Austrian border started. The colonel teased his friend saying—Dr. Rosenbloom, we are watching the inferiority of the Semitic race because now you certainly feel anguish, don't you? Dr. Rosenbloom replied calmly—Dear colonel, of course I admit I do feel anguish but why invoke the inferiority of one race and the superiority of the other? If you felt as much anguish as I now do you might have long ago run away. What matters, Frankl adds, is not the emotions we have but the attitude we take towards them. What matters is not whether we would want to take the money purse, but whether we could overcome the strong desire to take it.

III

This section concerns itself with the nature of human striving in Hasidism and logotherapy.

Hasidism—After Rabbi Uri Strelisker died, one of his disciples came to Rabbi Bunam who asked what specific character trait Rabbi Uri desired to instill in his hasidim. The hasid thought that Rabbi Uri desired to make his hasidim very humble. The rabbi would order a rich hasid to draw water at the pump and to bring in the pail on his shoulder, something the man would never have done at home. Rabbi Bunam said that he works differently. He explained with a parable. Three men convicted of a crime were locked in a dark cell. Two were intelligent, the third witless. When food was lowered to them, the witless person did not know how to take his share and would either break the plate or cut himself. One of the other prisoners tried to help him by rehearsing the necessary behavior, but the next day, a different food arrangement would be sent and the witless one would be perplexed. The third prisoner then remarked—why do you waste time teaching the fellow every day. Let me bore a hole into the wall to admit some light and then he will be able to help himself. Continued Rabbi Bunam—I try to admit into the human soul the awe and love of God. This is the light from which one can learn wise behavior in its totality and not trait by trait.

Logotherapy—There are different layers and dimensions to the human being but the spiritual dimension, which is the uniquely human one, is the higher dimension in that it includes the somatic and the psychic.

Hasidism—Rabbi Menachen Mendel of Vitebsk said that before the endlessness of God, the highest saint and the lowliest commoner are equal.

Logotherapy—The corollary to monotheism is "monoanthropism"—that is, the notion of the oneness of God may be paralleled by the notion of the oneness of humankind, all equal in their potential for good.

Hasidism—According to the Medzibozer, the individual has been placed in the world to contribute towards the improvement of the world. The hermit who avoids the society of people is inclined towards wickedness.

Logotherapy—The purpose of life is not achieved through self-actualization or self-realization, but rather through self-transcendence and orientation around "causes greater than oneself, and persons other than oneself."

Hasidism—The Kossover said that if one gives a donation to a poor person who then returns the donation asking for an even larger gift, agreement to this request brings boundless reward since such reaction is contrary to human nature.

Logotherapy—The key element in the human dynamics, along with self-transcendence, is "self-detachment"; that is, rising above oneself, thus becoming capable of judging oneself, and, if need be, opposing oneself.

Hasidism—According to the Kotzker every commandment should be performed with the proper intention, with one exception—humility.

Logotherapy—Certain actions of the individual demand the exercise of will. There are others which can only be realized in spontaneity if they are to be authentic. They cannot focus on the self for then such actions are stripped of their meaning. To be humble means, in a sense, to be oblivious of the self so that intending to be humble paradoxically makes humility impossible. Frankl also invokes the example of good conscience: fulfill your responsibilities, and good conscience will accrue; strive for good conscience, and it will elude you, because there is no ground for good conscience unless you have met your responsibilities.

Hasidism—Rabbi Bunam said—One should be careful of every move one makes in life just like the chess player is careful before making a move. Before any action is taken, one should anticipate whether there will be cause to regret the move.

Logotherapy—The leading maxim of existential analysis exhorts people to imagine that they are living now for the second time and had acted as wrongly the first time as they are about to act now.

Hasidism—The Lubliner said that he loves more a wicked person who is aware of his wickedness than he loves a good person who is aware of personal goodness.

Logotherapy—Life is a continual striving process towards reaching values. One must continually be aware of one's finiteness and the fact that there is so much more to achieve. Being always lags behind meaning, "meaning must be ahead of being; meaning sets the pace for being," as Frankl says.

Hasidism—The Lizensker Rebbe said that only God is perfect. Human actions must basically be partially defective. If one believes that one's good deed or holy study is thoroughly pure and perfect, then it is a sign that the individual is thoroughly bad.

Logotherapy—Only to the extent that man acknowledges his finiteness is he able to overcome it.

Hasidism—The Lubliner Rebbe was once asked why he took snuff in the midst of prayers even though interruptions were forbidden. The Lubliner in response told the story of a king who heard a street singer playing the violin. He liked the player and invited him to the king's court. The violinist would frequently break his routine because of a broken string. A member of the court finally asked the singer why he did not just restring his instrument to avoid interruptions. The street singer replied that obviously the king had many musicians with perfect instruments whom he could easily order to sing for him, but he prefers to hear me, which would indicate that he wants to hear my imperfect violin. Likewise, continued the Lubliner, God has an abundance of singing angels yet He has commanded that we pray to Him, so it is therefore clear that God is willing to tolerate our weaknesses.

Logotherapy—If all human beings were perfect then every human being would be the same and thus all human beings would be replaceable. There would be no individual uniqueness. It is precisely the imperfections within each individual which make for the differences and thus for the unique quality of every human being.

Hasidism—The Kaminker Rebbe tells that he once resolved to devote a whole day to the recitation of Psalms. Towards evening he was finishing when he was told that his rabbi, the Tzidnover Maggid, wanted to see him. The Kaminker said he would come as soon as he was finished but the Maggid told his messenger to insist that he come immediately. The Maggid asked the Kaminker why he did not come at first and the Kaminker told him the reason. The Maggid responded that he had called the Kaminker to make a collection for a poor Jew. Psalms can be sung by angels but only mortals can help the poor. Charity is greater than reciting the Psalms since angels cannot perform charity.

Logotherapy—The nature of meaning resides in the uniqueness of the individual, where the individual is irreplaceable, plus the uniqueness of the moment, which is irrepeatable. What others can do as well cannot signify a personal meaning, nor would it be meaningful to use the moment if we were immortal, and thus could postpone everything.

IV

This section focuses on value-orientation in Hasidism and logotherapy.

Hasidism—Rabbi Leib Saras questions the value of someone who studies Torah (Jewish law), but who nevertheless is full of pride and temper. Rather the person should be the Torah itself and other individuals should be able to learn how to behave from observing such an individual's conduct.

Logotherapy—Values cannot be taught. They must be ived.

Hasidism—According to the Kotzker Rebbe, there are three characters in the person about to perform a good deed. The one who says, "I shall do it soon," is poor character; the one who says, "I am ready to do it now," is of average quality; and the one who says, "I am doing it" is praiseworthy.

Logotherapy—Life is a task. The nature of the human task is not one which is realized through reflection, but through action. The human being is called upon to respond to the meaning offered by each life situation, and to actualize the meaning potential of the moment. The moment which has been wasted through failure to actualize meaning has been irrecoverably lost.

Hasidism—According to the "Yud" there are three character types among those who serve God—the one who labors all day but believes that nothing has been accomplished is at the highest point of merit; one who has done nothing to serve God and is aware of this is of average merit; one who is righteous and proud of this is least commendable. Such a person indulges in self deception and devotion to Torah and the commandments is wasted.

Logotherapy—A basic element of the human endeavor is the awareness of the infinite value possibility. One must constantly be aware that values are waiting to be actualized and that no matter how much has been achieved, there is always so much more left. One who fails to recognize this stagnates.

Hasidism—The "Yud" observed that one who does not feel one has improved in holiness during the day certainly has fallen back and was better the day before. The person always moves and never stands still. If one does not advance, one falls back.

Logotherapy—One must be aware of the value possibilities

constantly confronting the individual and behave responsibly towards this awareness. There is a subject/object tension within which the human being oscillates. One is constantly challenged to transcend the real state toward the ideal one. Failure to indulge in this dynamic essentially removes the individual from the human dimension and is thus a regression.

Hasidism—The Gerer Rebbe once asked a young man if he had learned Torah. Just a little, responded the man, to which the Gerer retorted—That is all that anyone has ever learned of the Torah.

Logotherapy—Life offers infinite possibilities. The individual is finite and therefore can never exhaust the infinite possibilities. But the individual must try: "Things are bad," Frankl says. "But unless we do our best to improve them, everything will become worse."[3]

Hasidism—The Sassover Rebbe used to go to county fairs and help people in need. On one occasion, some cattlemen left their animals standing in the marketplace, exceedingly thirsty, whilst they went to attend to their affairs. When the Sassover Rebbe saw this, he brought a bucket and gave the calves to drink. One dealer who came back from an errand and saw this mistook the Sassover for a hired hand and commanded the Sassover to give water to his cattle. The Sassover gladly obeyed and after he gave the animals to drink was given a coin by the dealer. He refused to accept it, saying—Go away, I did not feed the cattle because you ordered me but because God ordered me, God who commands us to be merciful to God's creatures.

Logotherapy—Do not do things for thereby gaining power or pleasure. Do things for their own sake, or for the sake of another person.

V

This section reflects on the element of meaning in Hasidism and logotherapy.

Hasidism—A young man came to the Riziner Rebbe wanting to receive rabbinical ordination. The Riziner asked the fellow about his daily conduct. The young man said that he always dressed in white, drank only water, placed tacks in his shoes for self-mortification, rolled naked in the snow and ordered the synagogue caretaker to give him forty stripes daily on his bare back. Just at that moment, a white horse entered the Rebbe's courtyard, drank water, and began rolling in the snow. See, said the Rebbe to the young man, this creature is white, drinks only water, has nails in its shoes, roll in the snow and surely gets more than forty stripes a day, yet is nothing but a horse.

Logotherapy—It is not the act itself which is crucial. It is the meaning with which the act is invested, the human quality which gives it value.

Hasidism—The Baal Shem Tov recommended that it is desirable for a person to frequently interrupt one's occupation for a short pause and concentrate upon the awe of God, even if involved in a sacred occupation.

Logotherapy—The individual should not act along the lines of rote mechanistic behavior but rather orient around meaning and purpose, even in endeavors which on their own may be meaningful. Approaching them mechanistically eliminates the meaning perspective. The awareness of why one performs an action greatly affects the how.

Hasidism—Rabbi Leib Saras said that he did not journey to Rabbi Dov Baer of Mezeritz to learn interpretations of the Torah, but rather to study how Rabbi Dov Baer tied his shoelaces and took off his shoes. What worth are the meanings given to the Torah? It is in one's actions, one's speech, one's bearing and loyalty to God that one makes manifest the Torah.

Logotherapy—This is a "man in the street" type of orientation which emphasizes that it is not the ivory tower dialectic which is crucial but the daily lifestyle which is lived meaningfully by virtue of the "pre-reflective ontological self-understanding," by which term Frankl ultimately means the "wisdom of the heart."[4]

Hasidism—A person once approached the Kotzker Rebbe asking that the rabbi pray that the individual's sons would study the Torah diligently. The Kotzker replied—If your sons will see that you are a diligent student, they will follow your example. However, if you neglect your own studies and just wish that your sons study, they will do just as you do when they grow up. They will neglect Torah study but will want that their sons study.

Logotherapy—Meaning can never be pushed off into the next generation. What is meaningless in itself does not become meaningful by extending its existence over generations. To think that by having children one has found true meaning would be to push off meaning into the next generation, but each generation would then do this, ad infinitum. Instead, meaning must be found in the here and now and children then will carry that meaning into future generations. Frankl himself tells the story of a man who bought a parrot and tried to get the parrot to call him "Daddy," but the parrot did not co-operate. The owner, in frustration, punished the uncooperative parrot by locking it overnight in a hen house. In the morning, when he came to take the parrot from its prison, all but one of the chickens had been killed by the parrot. The parrot was holding the lone surviving chicken in its claws and shouting incessantly—"Call me Daddy! Call me Daddy! Call me Daddy!" The parrot behaved in as authoritarian a manner as its owner, and, like the owner, received no co-operation from those of whom the demands were made.

Hasidism—The Porissover Rebbe said that if a person is poor and meek, it is easy for that individual to be joyful as that individual has nothing to be afraid of losing.

Logotherapy—One can overcome fear by confronting fear-arousing situations, even "paradoxically" wishing to happen what one had been afraid of all along.

VI

This section projects attitudes to despair, suffering, and death in Hasidism and logotherapy.

Hasidism—The Kobriner Rebbe tells that when he was a young boy there was a famine in which the poor went from village to village begging for food. Some came to his mother's house and she began to bake for them. Some of the poor beggars became impatient and started insulting the rabbi's mother, who began to cry. Still a boy, the future Kobriner Rebbe said to his mother—Why should you be bothered by their insults? In fact, their insults make it possible for you to help them with a pure heart and to do a good deed in perfect spirit. If they had praised you, you might have done the good deed in order to gain their praises and this would have made your deed less praiseworthy than now, when you are doing it entirely in fulfillment of God's command and for the sake of serving God.

Logotherapy—The individual, in all situations, even in situations of despair, can overcome the despair through taking the proper attitude to the situation, thereby finding a meaning to the very despair.

Hasidism—The Lubliner Rebbe commented that God becomes attentive to the person who sings in the midst of personal troubles and accepts these troubles good-naturedly and with laughter.

Logotherapy—Adverse circumstances are not meaningless but offer the possibility to fulfill even the deepest possible meaning; that is, "to turn tragedy into a personal triumph, to turn one's predicament into a human achievement."[5]

Hasidism—Rabbi Isaac Meyer of Ger had thirteen sons, all of whom died. At the death of the youngest, it was impossible to comfort his wife. Rabbi Isaac Meyer said to her —Our sons have not died in vain. If a misfortune such as this should befall others, they will remember that Isaac Meyer lost thirteen holy sons and so they will not feel angry against God.

Logotherapy—The meaning of life is unconditional, even in cases of intense suffering. There is a meaning to life in the suffering which makes the suffering bearable. Despair associated with suffering exists only because one fails to see a meaning in the suffering itself.

Hasidism—When Rabbi Bunam was lying on his death bed, his wife cried bitter tears. He said to her—Why do you cry? All my life has been given to me merely so that I should learn how to die.

Logotherapy—Without death, human life cannot be complete. And death is another challenge to take a proper attitude, and, by so doing, "rise above, and grow beyond oneself."[6] A good death is the culmination of a good life.

Hasidism—The Gerer asked why a person fears dying. Is not death a return to God in Heaven? The reason for the fear is that in the future world, one gains a clear perspective of all one's deeds on earth. The individual who becomes aware of the senseless things committed on earth cannot abide the self and in that awareness inheres Hell.

Logotherapy—It is only the individual who has not lived properly who is afraid to die. If life is a "becoming" process then in death one has attained "being."[7] If one has lived a complete life then death as a natural culmination of life is easier to accept.

Hasidism—The Belzer Rebbe heard a man express a wish to die like a good Jew. The Belzer retorted—You should rather desire to live like a good Jew and it will follow in consequence that you will die a good Jew.

Logotherapy—"Man's past is his true future."[8] What has been achieved can never be erased.

VII

This section offers a comparison of the nature of love in Hasidism and logotherapy.

Hasidism—Rabbi Shlomo Karliner said that God treats a person in the same way that one treats one's children. If you do not neglect your children, God will not neglect you.

Logotherapy—Love is not something which can be demanded. The individual lives out humanness best by transcending the self, by immersing the self in the other. The individual thereby generates a pattern of concern for the other which, in turn, brings out the best in the couple.

Hasidism—Rabbi Moshe Leib of Sassov said that to truly love means to know what brings pain to your friend.

Logotherapy—True love involves self-transcendence towards the "thou" and being concerned about the other. The true fulfillment of the self comes via fulfilling the other individual.

Hasidism—Moshe Leib Sassover sat at the bedside of the sick in his city, nursing and caring for them. He said that one who cannot suck the matter from the boils of a child stricken with the plague has not reached to one-half the ultimate level of love for one's fellow beings.

Logotherapy—True love involves "forgetting oneself by giving oneself."[9]

Hasidism—The Berditschever said that one who serves God out of fear never forgets one's own existence but still fears God, but the one who serves out of love forgets about the self entirely.

Logotherapy—In true love, one does not focus on the self, but one is immersed in the other.

VIII

This section presents perspectives on work and material gain in Hasidism and logotherapy.

Hasidism—According to the Kotzker, the prohibition against making idols includes the prohibition against making idols out of the commandments. One should not think that the purpose of a commandment resides in the outer form and that the inner meaning should not be considered relevant. Insted, the opposite position should be adopted.

Logotherapy—Even in the act of doing that which is very meaningful, such as the practice of medicine, it is not the actual practice which is most meaningful as much as the attitude with which one approaches the profession and the human quality with which one invests the work.

Hasidism—The Baal Shem Tov once went with his son to visit the ailing rabbi of Medziboz. The son was admiring a cabinet full of silverware. The Baal Shem Tov said to his son —You think in your heart that this silverware is in the wrong place and that it should be in your father's house. You are half right and half wrong. The silverware is in its wrong place, but not because it is not with us. It should rather be given away as charity instead of shining here as futile ornaments.

Logotherapy—The will to meaning is the basic human striving. The will to power confuses the means with the end itself. Power is not an end in itself nor is the acquisition of wealth an end in itself. Instead these are means towards the actualization of values.

Hasidism—Rabbi Nachum Tzernobiler said that if it is a choice between poverty and wealth, he would always choose poverty because poverty is a shield against egotism and any other spiritual evil. It is least costly and most easily obtainable. It does not have to struggle with jealousy and competition. It need not respond to questions or suspicions and is understood without comment or explanation. Continues Rabbi Nachum—I beg of you, my good friends, do not deprive me of this great treasure.

Logotherapy—It is not the circumstance as such which is

either meaningful or meaningless, it is rather the approach one takes to that situation. The right attitude can transmute a reality from the suffering dimension into the dimension of meaning.

Hasidism—A hasid once complained to the Kotzker that he was so engrossed in his business that he could not spend time on the study of Talmud and Hasidism. The Kotzker explained to the hasid that God wished to benefit Israel and therefore gave them many commandments. But, what is the benefit of having the responsibility for many commandments? It is, in fact, a hardship for it would have been much easier to have just a few precepts which could easily have been observed. The answer is that the variety of precepts allows individuals in different areas to do God's bidding. A farmer, a planter, a house builder, etc., each has specific obligations and therefore can do God's work. The merchant, by being honest, not overcharging and not deceiving, pleases God.

Logotherapy—There is meaning in every situation. The notion of unconditional meaning in life asserts that no situation is devoid of meaning. Even where one is confronted with an unavoidable suffering, one may, through a proper attitude, give that situation its meaning quality.

IX

Hasidism, it will be readily apparent, contains some very profound ideas, but these profound ideas are essentially very simple ideas. They strike at the very core of human existence. The same may be said of the philosophy of logotherapy as well as its clinical approach.

It is not relevant whether the hasidic sages were logotherapists or whether logotherapists are hasidim. The key element is that hasidic sages could easily practice logotherapy and logotherapists could easily be hasidim. Their respective outlooks, attitudes, and approaches are strikingly similar. Moreover, the hasidic masters, unbeknown to them, often practiced what may be termed "meta-clinical therapy," sometimes of a one-to-one nature, sometimes of a group nature. They attempted, by re-orienting distorted thinking, to solve the problems of the masses. That, ironically, is logotherapy's greatest strength.

CONCLUSION

After having wrestled with problems of the immediate and the ultimate, it remains as the concluding task to confront the crucial question of questions—What is the meaning and purpose of life?—in effect, to address the problem of the quest for ultimate meaning.

One is likely to be disappointed with the response—there is no answer. Yet, any attempt to reduce a problem of infinite proportions to finite terms must be considered suspect.

Frankl, as has been shown, proposes the notion of super-meaning as suggestive of the reality that we can never really know and grasp the ultimate meaning, as it is beyond us, or a super-meaning.

Logotherapy opens the door to ultimate meaning, it points the way toward that quest. But it offers no answers, only the possibilities. Existentially, we are in a situation of becoming. Theologically, we are in a situation of perpetual quest.

The philosophy and psychology of logotherapy, interrelated as they are, show how concern for the ultimate has great impact on the immediate. The quest for ultimate meaning is a fertile context for realizing the meaning of the moment.

The ultimate, however, remains unanswered, even unanswerable. One might add that anything more would detract rather than add to life. For it is in the state of seeking, reaching, growing that we come across the micro-meanings which inspire toward the macro-meaning. One who has all the answers has, at the same time, no motivation to seek, to reach, to grow.

There are no ultimate answers in the immediate, thus guaranteeing the continuing quest. To employ a piece of Talmudic reasoning, *the quest for ultimate meaning* is not the question; it is the response. It is to find by seeking, to find more by seeking more, but never to find all; instead, actualizing as much as is possible in one's finite life, always in quest.

To borrow a phrase used by Frankl, "Sometimes the unfinisheds are the most beautiful symphonies," and this, because their music never ends.

REFERENCES

ANSEL, A. *Judaism and psychology.* New York: Philip Feldheim, Inc., 1969.

ARNOLD, M. B., and GASSON, A. *The human person.* New York: Ronald Press, 1954.

ASCHER, L. M. Paradoxical intention: A review of preliminary research. *The International forum for Logotherapy,* 1978-1979, 1 (1), 18-21.

BIRNBAUM, F. Frankl's existential psychology from the viewpoint of individual psychology. *Journal of Individual Psychology,* 1961, *17,* 162-166.

BULKA, R. P. Logotherapy and judaism—Some philosophical comparisons. *Tradition,* 1972, *12*(3-4), 72-89.

BULKA, R. P. The ecumenical ingredient in logotherapy. *Journal of Ecumenical Studies,* 1974, *11*(1).

BURSTEIN, A. (Ed.). *The worlds of Norman Salit.* New York: Bloch, 1966.

BURTON, A. (Ed.). *Modern psychotherapeutic practice: Innovations in technique.* Palo Alto: Science and Behavior Books, 1965.

FABRY, J. B. *The pursuit of meaning: Logotherapy applied to life.* Boston: Beacon Press, 1968.

FOX, D. A. Logotherapy and religion. *Religion in Life,* 1965, *31,* 235-244.

FRANKL, V. E. *Die psychotherapie in der praxis.* Vienna: Franz Deuticke, 1947.

FRANKL, V. E. Logos and existence in psychotherapy. *American Journal of Psychotherapy,* 1953, *7,* 8-15.

FRANKL, V. E. The concept of man in psychotherapy. *Pastoral Psychology,* 1955, *6,* 16-26.

FRANKL, V. E. The will to meaning. *Journal of Pastoral Care,* 1958, *12,* 82-88.

FRANKL, V. E. The spiritual dimension in existential analysis and logotherapy. *Journal of Individual Psychology,* 1959, *15,* 157-165.

FRANKL, V. E. Beyond self-actualization and self-expression. *Journal of Existential Psychiatry*, 1960, *1*, 5-20.
FRANKL, V. E. Religion and existential psychotherapy. *Gordon Review*, 1961, *6*, 2-10.
FRANKL, V. E. Basic concepts of logotherapy. *Journal of Existential Psychiatry*, 1962, *3*, 111-118.
FRANKL, V. E. Psychiatry and man's quest for meaning. *Journal of Religion and Health*, 1962, *1*, 93-103.
FRANKL, V. E. *Man's search for meaning: An introduction to logotherapy.* New York: Washington Square Press, 1963.
FRANKL, V. E. Self-transcendence as a human phenomenon. *Journal of Humanistic Psychology*, 1966, *6*(2), 97-106.
FRANKL, V. E. *Three lectures.* Transcription of a tape printed as a manuscript. Brandeis, California: Brandeis Institute, 1966.
FRANKL, V. E. Time and responsibility. *Existential Psychiatry*, 1966, *1*, 361-366.
FRANKL, V. E. *The doctor and the soul: From psychotherapy to logotherapy.* New York: Bantam Books, 1967.
FRANKL, V. E. *Psychotherapy and existentialism: Selected papers on logotherapy.* New York: Simon and Schuster, 1968.
FRANKL, V. E. *The will to meaning: Foundations and applications of logotherapy.* New York: World Publishing Co., 1969.
FRANKL, V. E. *Comments of Dr. Viktor E. Frankl on logotherapy and the talmud.* San Diego: Logotherapy Institute of of United States International University, 1970. (Contains Frankl's reactions to an unpublished work by Reuven P. Bulka.)
FRANKL, V. E. Determinism and humanism. *Humanitas (Journal of the Institute of Man)*, 1971, *7*, 23-36.
FRANKL, V. E. The Depersonalization of sex. *Synthesis,* Spring 1974, *1*, 7-11.
FRANKL, V. E. Paradoxical intention and de-reflection. *Psychotherapy: Theory, Research and Practice,* Fall 1975, *12*(3), 226-237.
FRANKL, V. E. *The unconscious god: Psychotherapy and theology.* New York: Simon and Schuster, 1975.
FRANKL, V. E. Lecture given at the inauguration of the Frankl Library and Memorabilia. Berkeley, California: Graduate Theological Union, February 12, 1977.

FRANKL, V. E. *The unheard cry for meaning: Psychotherapy and humanism.* New York: Simon and Schuster, 1978.

FRIEDMAN, M. Aiming at the self: The paradox of encounter and the human potential movement. *Journal of Humanistic Psychology,* 1976, *16*(2), 5-34.

GOLDSTEIN, A. & FOA, E. B. (Eds.). *Handbook of behavioral interventions.* New York: John Wiley, 1979.

GROLLMAN, E. A. The logotherapy of Viktor E. Frankl. *Judaism,* 1965, *14*(1), 22-38.

GROSSMAN, N. The rabbi and the doctor of the soul. *Jewish Spectator,* January, 1969, *34*(1), 8-12.

HALPERIN, I. *Messengers from the dead: Literature of the holocaust.* Philadelphia: The Westminster Press, no date.

HAROLD, P. *The shining stranger: An unorthodox interpretation of Jesus and his mission.* New York: The Wayfarer Press, 1967.

THE HOLY SCRIPTURES (2 vols.). Philadelphia: Jewish Publication Society, 1917.

KUBLER-ROSS, E. *On death and dying.* New York: Macmillan, 1970.

LESLIE, R.C. *Jesus and logotherapy: The ministry of Jesus as interpreted through the psychotherapy of Viktor Frankl.* New York and Nashville: Abingdon Press, 1965.

LETTER, S. S. (Ed.). *New prospects for the small liberal arts college.* New York: Teachers College Press, 1968.

MAIMONIDES, M. MISHNAH TORAH (6 vols.). New York: M. P. Press, 1962.

MASLOW, A. M. Comments on Dr. Frankl's paper. *Journal of Humanistic Psychology,* 1966, *6*(2), 107-112.

MAY, R. *Man's search for himself.* New York: W. W. Norton, 1953.

MAY, R., ANGEL, E., & ELLENBERGER, H. F. (Eds.). *Existence: A new dimension in psychiatry and psychology.* New York: Simon and Schuster, 1958.

MAY, R. (Ed.). *Existential psychology.* New York: Random House, 1961.

MAY, R. *Psychology and the human dilemma.* Princeton: D. Van Nostrand, 1967.

THE MIDRASH. H. Friedman & Maurice Simon (Eds.). London: Soncino Press, 1961.

MIDRASH TANCHUMA (2 vols.). New York: Ateres Publications, 1969.
NEWMAN, L. I. *The hasidic anthology: Tales and teachings of the hasidim.* New York: Schocken Books, 1963.
PATTERSON, C. H. *Theories of counseling and psychotherapy.* New York: Harper & Row, 1966.
RUBENSTEIN, R. L. *The religious imagination: A study in psychoanalysis and jewish theology.* Boston: Beacon Press, 1971.
RUITENBECK, H. M. (Ed.). *Death: Interpretations.* New York: Dell Publishing Co., 1969.
SAHAKIAN, W. S. & SAHAKIAN, B. J. Logotherapy as a personality theory. *The Israel Annals of Psychiatry and Related Disciplines*, September 1972, *10*(3), 230-244.
SOLYOM, L., GARZA-PEREZ, J., LEDWIDGE, B. L. & SOLYOM, C. Paradoxical intention in the treatment of obsessive thoughts: A pilot study. *Comprehensive Psychiatry*, 1972, 13(3), 291-297.
STANDAL, S. W. & CORSINI, R. J. (Eds.). *Critical incidents in psychotherapy.* Englewood Cliffs: Prentice-Hall, 1959.
STRAUSS, E. W. (Ed.). *Phenomenology: Pure and applied.* Pittsburgh: Duquesne University Press, 1964.
THE TALMUD (18 vols.). I. Epstein (Ed.). London: Soncino Press, 1961.
TWEEDIE, D. F. *Logotherapy and the christian faith: An evaluation of Frankl's existential approach to psychotherapy.* Grand Rapids: Baker Book House, 1965.
UNGERSMA, A. J. *The search for meaning: A new approach in psychotherapy and pastoral psychology.* Philadelphia: Westminster Press, 1968.
WEISS, R. S. *Marital separation.* New York: Basic Books, 1975.

FOOTNOTES

SECTION 1
CHAPTER ONE
IS LOGOTHERAPY AUTHORITARIAN?

[1] Rollo May, Ernest Angel, & Henri F. Ellenberger (Eds). *Existence: A New Dimension in Psychology* (New York: Simon and Schuster, 1958).

[2] May, (Ed.). *Existential Psychology* (New York, Random House, 1961), p. 42.

[3] Viktor E. Frankl, *The Unconscious God: Psychotherapy and Theology* (New York: Simon and Schuster, 1975), p. 121.

[4] May, *Psychology and the Human Dilemma* (Princeton: D. Van Nostrand, 1967), p. 180.

[5] Frankl, *The Doctor and the Soul: From Psychotherapy to Logotherapy* (New York: Bantam Books, 1967), p. 222. (Originally published in German in 1946).

[6] *Ibid.*, p. 167.

[7] *Ibid.*, p. 109.

[8] Frankl, *The Unconscious God*, p. 141.

[9] May, *Man's Search for Himself* (New York: W. W. Norton, 1953).

[10] Frankl, *The Unconscious God*, p. 79.

[11] Frankl, The Philosophical Foundations of Logotherapy. In Erwin W. Strauss (Ed.), *Phenomenology: Pure and Applied* (Pittsburgh, Duquesne University Press, 1964), p. 43.

[12] May, *Psychology and the Human Dilemma*, p. 174.

[13] *Ibid.*, p. 175.

[14] Frankl, *The Will to Meaning: Foundations and Applications of Logotherapy* (New York: World Publishing Company, 1969), p. 62.

[15] May, *Psychology and the Human Dilemma*, p. 175.

[16] Frankl, *The Doctor and the Soul*, p. 61.

[17] *Ibid.*, p. 91.

[18] Frankl, "Religion and Existential Psychotherapy," *Gordon Review*, Vol. 6 (1961), p. 8.

[19] Frankl, *The Doctor and the Soul*, p. 180.

[20] May, *Man's Search for Himself*, p. 137.

[21] *Ibid.*, pp. 188-189.

[22] Frankl, *Psychotherapy and Existentialism: Selected Papers on Logotherapy* (New York: Simon and Schuster, 1968), p. 55.

[23] *Ibid.*, p. 16.

[24] *Ibid.*, p. 64.

[25] Frankl, "The Spiritual Dimension in Existential Analysis and Logotherapy," *Journal of Individual Psychology*, Vol. 15 (1959), p. 158.

[26] Frankl, *Man's Search for Meaning: An Introduction to Logotherapy* (New York: Washington Square Press, 1963), p. 175.

[27] Cf. Abraham Maslow, "Comments on Dr. Frankl's Paper," *Journal of Humanistic Psychology*, Vol. 6, No. 2 (1966), pp. 107-112.

[28] Cf. Maurice Friedman, "Aiming at the Self: The Paradox of En-

counter and the Human Potential Movement," *Journal of Humanistic Psychology*, Vol. 16, No. 2 (1976), pp. 5-34.

[29] Frankl, "Beyond Self-Actualization and Self-Expression," *Journal of Existential Psychiatry*, Vol. 1 (1960), p. 14.

[30] Frankl, *The Doctor and the Soul*, p. xii.

[31] In a personal conversation, Frankl related to me a conversation he had with Heidegger, in which he confronted Heidegger with the fact that in America he is interpreted along the lines of subjectivism. Enraged, Heidegger exclaimed, "I am in no way a subjectivist."

[32] Frankl, *The Unconscious God*, p. 123.

[33] Frankl, *Man's Search for Meaning*, p. 173.

[34] Frankl, *The Unconscious God*, p. 141.

[35] Frankl, *The Doctor and the Soul*, pp. 223-224.

[36] Frankl, *The Unconscious God*, p. 123.

[37] Frankl, *Man's Search for Meaning*, p. 174.

[38] Frankl, *The Unconscious God*, p. 123.

[39] Frankl, "Fragments from the Logotherapeutic Treatment of Four Cases." In Arthur Burton (Ed.), *Modern Psychoterapeutic Practice: Innovations in Technique* (Palo Alto, California: Science and Behavior Books, 1965), pp. 368-370.

[40] Godfryd Kaczanowski, "Introduction and Epilogue to Fragments from the Logotherapeutic Treatment of Four Cases." In Arthur Burton (Ed.), *op., cit.*, p. 376.

[41] Frankl, *The Doctor and the Soul*, p. 230.

CHAPTER II
PARADOXICAL INTENTION AND DE-REFLECTION

[1] Viktor E. Frankl, "Paradoxical Intention and Dereflection," *Psychotherapy: Theory, Research and Practice*, Vol. 12, No. 3 (1975), pp. 226-237.

[2] Frankl, *The Unheard Cry for Meaning: Psychotherapy and Humanism* (New York: Simon and Schuster, 1978), pp. 114-162.

[3] L. Solyom, J. Garza-Perez, B. L. Ledwidge, and C. Solyom, "Paradoxical Intention in the Treatment of Obsessive Thoughts: A Pilot Study," *Comprehensive Psychiatry*, Vol. 13, No. 3 (1972), 291-297.

[4] L. Michael Ascher, "Paradoxical Intention." In A. Goldstein & E. B. Foa (Eds.), *Handbook of Behavioral Intervention* (New York: John Wiley, 1979).

[5] Ascher, "Paradoxical Intention: A Review of Preliminary Research," *The International Forum for Logotherapy*, Vol. 1, No. 1 (Winter 1978 — Spring 1979), pp. 18-21.

SECTION 2
CHAPTER III
THE ECUMENICAL INGREDIENT IN LOGOTHERAPY

[1] Viktor E. Frankl, *The Doctor and the Soul: From Psychotherapy to Logotherapy* (New York: Bantam Books, 1967), p. 230.

[2] Frankl, *Man's Search for Meaning: An Introduction to Logotherapy* (New York: Washington Square Press, 1963), p. 154.

³ Frankl, *The Doctor and the Soul*, pp. ix-x.
⁴ Frankl, "The Philosophical Foundations of Logotherapy." In Erwin W. Strauss (Ed.), *Phenomenology: Pure and Applied* (Pittsburgh: Duquesne University Press, 1964), p. 43.
⁵ *Ibid.*, p. 44.
⁶ Frankl, *The Doctor and the Soul*, p. xvii.
⁷ Frankl, "The Philosophical Foundations of Logotherapy," *op. cit.*, pp. 47-49.
⁸ Frankl, *Man's Search for Meaning*, p. 175.
⁹ Frankl, "The Spiritual Dimension in Existential Analysis and Logotherapy," *Journal of Individual Psychology*, Vol. 15 (1959), p. 158.
¹⁰ Frankl, *The Doctor and the Soul*, pp. 34-36. See further, pp. 47-48, where Frankl associates the three values—creative, experiential, and attitudinal—with Judaism, Protestantism, and Christianity.
¹¹ Frankl, *Comments of Dr. Viktor E. Frankl on Logotherapy and the Talmud* (San Diego: Logotherapy Institute of United States International University, 1970), pp. 1-2.
¹² Frankl, "The Philosophical Foundations of Logotherapy," *op. cit.*, p. 54.
¹³ Frankl, *Man's Search for Meaning*, p. 115.
¹⁴ *Ibid.*, p. 187.
¹⁵ Frankl, *The Doctor and the Soul*, p. 47.
¹⁶ Frankl, *Man's Search for Meaning*, pp. 141-142.
¹⁷ Frankl, *Comments of Dr. Viktor E. Frankl on Logotherapy and the Talmud*, p. 14.
¹⁸ Frankl, *Handbuch der Neurosenlehre und Psychotherapie* (Wien: Urban and Schwartzenberg, 1957), p. 694, quoted by Donald F. Tweedie, Jr., in *Logotherapy and the Christian Faith: An Evaluation of Frankl's Existential Approach to Psychotherapy* (Grand Rapids, Michigan: Baker Book House, 1965), p. 62.
¹⁹ Frankl, *Logos und Existenz* (Wien: Amandus Verlag, 1951), p. 64, quoted by Tweedie, *op. cit.*, p. 34.
²⁰ Frankl, "Religion and Existential Psychotherapy," *Gordon Review*, Vol. 6 (1961), p. 5. See also, Frankl, "Contributions." In S. W. Standal and and R. J. Corsini (Eds.), *Critical Incidents in Psychotherapy* (Englewood Cliffs, N.J.: Prentice-Hall, 1959), pp. 8-11.
²¹ Frankl, "Psychiatry and Man's Quest for Meaning," *Journal of Religion and Health*, Vol. 1 (1962), p. 94.
²² Frankl, "The Philosophical Foundations of Logotherapy," *op. cit.*, p. 55.
²³ Frankl, "Basic Concepts of Logotherapy," *Journal of Existential Psychiatry*, Vol. 3 (1962), pp. 116-117.
²⁴ Aaron J. Ungersma, *The Search for Meaning: A New Approach in Psychotherapy and Pastoral Psychology* (Philadelphia: Westminster Press, 1968), p. 22.
²⁵ Tweedie, *op. cit.*, p. 151.
²⁶ C. H. Patterson, *Theories of Counseling and Psychotherapy* (New York: Harper and Row, 1966), p. 481.
²⁷ Frankl, "The Concept of Man in Psychotherapy," *Pastoral Psychology*, Vol. 6 (1955), p. 20. See also, Joseph B. Fabry, *The Pursuit*

of Meaning: Logotherapy Applied to Life (Boston: Beacon Press, 1968), p. 34.

[28] Ferdinand Birnbaum, "Frankl's Existential Psychology from the Viewpoint of Individual Psychology," *Journal of Individual Psychology,* Vol. 17 (1961), p. 163.

[29] Magda B. Arnold and John A. Gasson, *The Human Person* (New York: Ronald Press, 1954), p. 486.

[30] *Ibid.*, p. 485.

[31] Tweedie, *op. cit.*, p. 161.

[32] *Ibid.*, pp. 161-162.

[33] *Ibid.*, p. 162.

[34] *Ibid.*, p. 163.

[35] Robert C. Leslie, *Jesus and Logotherapy: The Ministry of Jesus as Interpreted through the Psychotherapy of Viktor Frankl* (New York and Nashville: Abingdon Press, 1965), p. 144.

[36] *Ibid.*, p. 22, p. 72, pp. 121-122, p. 93.

[37] Douglas A. Fox, "Logotherapy and Religion," *Religion in Life,* Vol. 34 (1965), pp. 235-244.

[38] Ungersma, *The Search for Meaning,* p. 110.

[39] Earl A. Grollman, "The Logotherapy of Viktor E. Frankl," *Judaism,* Vol. 14 (1965), pp. 22-38.

[40] Frankl, *The Will to Meaning: Foundations and Applications of Logotherapy* (New York: The World Publishing Company, 1969), p. 55.

[41] Leo Baeck, quoted by Frankl, *Three Lectures.* Transcription of a Tape Printed as a Manuscript (Brandeis, Calif.: Brandeis Institute, 1966), Lecture 1, p. 1,

[42] Abraham Amsel, *Judaism and Psychology* (New York: Philip Feldheim, Inc., 1969), p. 182.

[43] Nathan Grossman, "The Rabbi and the Doctor of the Soul," *The Jewish Spectator,* Vol. 34 (1969), pp. 8-12.

[44] Norman Salit, "Judaism and Psychotherapy," in Abraham Burstein (Ed.), *The Worlds of Norman Salit* (New York: Bloch Publishing, 1966), pp. 288-308.

[45] Reuven P. Bulka, "Logotherapy and Judaism—Some Philosophical Comparisons," *Tradition,* Vol. 12, No. 3-4 (1972). pp. 72-89.

[46] Frankl, *Comments of Dr. Viktor E. Frankl on Logotherapy and the Talmud,* pp. 10-13.

[47] *Ibid.*, p. 14.

[48] Preston Harold, *The Shining Stranger: An Unorthodox Interpretation of Jesus and His Mission* (New York: The Wayfarer Press, 1967), p. 381.

[49] Frankl, *The Will to Meaning,* p. 143.

[50] Frankl, *The Doctor and the Soul,* p. 25.

[51] Frankl, "Determinism and Humanism," *Humanitas: Journal of the Institute of Man,* Vol. 7, No. 1 (1971), p. 35.

[52] Grossman, "The Rabbi and the Doctor of the Soul," *op. cit.*, p. 11.

[53] Frankl, *Three Lectures,* Lecture 3, p. 7.

[54] *Ibid.*

[55] Frankl, *The Will to Meaning,* p. 154.

[56] Fabry, *The Pursuit of Meaning,* p. 182.

[57] Grollman, "The Logotherapy of Viktor E. Frankl," *op. cit.*, 37.
[58] Frankl, *Comments of Dr. Viktor E. Frankl on Logotherapy and the Talmud*, p. 8.
[59] *Ibid.*, p. 4.
[60] Frankl, *The Will to Meaning*, p. 150.
[61] Frankl, "Contributions," *op. cit.*, p. 10
[62] Frankl, *Comments of Dr. Viktor E. Frankl on Logotherapy and the Talmud*, pp. 4-5.
[63] There are some important implications for general theology in the statements of Frankl. In effect, he projects a world with everything going in the same general direction, both atheism and religiosity. The direction being infinite, and the ultimate unknown and unknowable, the so-called non-religious live peacefully without filling in the unknown. Filling in the unknown is the specific aim of the religious, but even that, to Frankl, is still conjecture. Ultimately, even in religion it is unknown and remains a matter of trust. Carrying this to an extreme would imply we are all believers in terms of attitude, and non-believers in terms of certitude. The broader implications of this extension for theology are, of course, intriguing, but beyond the scope of this paper.
[64] Frankl, *Comments of Dr. Viktor E. Frankl on Logotherapy and the Talmud*, pp. 4-5.
[65] See *The Will to Meaning*, p. 98, where Frankl coins this term and develops its meaning.

CHAPTER IV
IS LOGOTHERAPY A SPIRITUAL THERAPY?

[1] Viktor E. Frankl, *The Doctor and the Soul: From Psychotherapy to Logotherapy* (New York: Bantam Books, 1967), p. xvi.
[2] Gordon W. Allport, "Comments on Earlier Chapters." In Rollo May (Ed.), *Existential Psychology* (New York: Random House, 1961), p. 97.
[3] Frankl, *The Unconscious God: Psychotherapy and Theology* (New York: Simon and Schuster, 1975), p. 81.
[4] *Ibid.*, pp. 90-91.
[5] *Ibid.*, p. 84.
[6] Frankl, "Psychiatry and Man's Quest for Meaning," *Journal of Religion and Health*, Vol. 1 (1962), p. 94.
[7] Frankl, *Man's Search for Meaning: An Introduction to Logotherapy* (New York: Washington Square Press, 1963), p. 154.
[8] Frankl, "The Philosophical Foundations of Logotherapy." In Erwin W. Strauss (Ed.), *Phenomenology: Pure and Applied* (Pittsburgh: Duquesne University Press, 1964), p. 43.
[9] Frankl, *The Doctor and the Soul*, p. 61.
[10] Frankl, *The Unconscious God*, p. 100.
[11] Frankl, *The Will to Meaning: Foundations and Applications of Logotherapy* (New York: World Publishing Company, 1969), p. 63.
[12] Frankl, *Man's Search for Meaning*, p. 172.
[13] Frankl, *The Doctor and the Soul*, p. 91.
[14] Frankl, *The Unconscious God*, p. 128.

15 Frankl, *The Doctor and the Soul*, p. 65.
16 *Ibid.*, p. 52.
17 *Ibid.*, p. 27.
18 Frankl, "Time and Responsibility," *Existential Psychiatry*, Vol. 1 (1966), p. 365.
19 Frankl, *The Doctor and the Soul*, p. 95.
20 Frankl, *The Will to Meaning*, p. 140.
21 Frankl, "The Philosophical Foundations of Logotherapy," *op. cit.*, p. 55.
22 Frankl, *The Unconscious God*, p. 26.
23 *Ibid.*, p. 31
24 *Ibid.*, p. 55.
25 Frankl, "Contributions." In S. W. Standal & R. J. Corsini (Eds.), *Critical Incidents in Psychotherapy* (Englewood Cliffs, New Jersey: Prentice-Hall, 1959), p. 10.
26 Frankl, *The Unconscious God*, p. 72.
27 Frankl, *Man's Search for Meaning*, pp. 141-142.
28 Frankl, *Comments of Dr. Viktor E. Frankl on Logotherapy and the Talmud* (San Diego: Logotherapy Institute of United States International University, 1970), pp. 1-2.
29 Ferdinand Birnbaum, "Frankl's Existential Psychology from the Viewpoint of Individual Psychology," *Journal of Individual Psychology*, Vol. 17 (1961), p. 163.
30 Magda B. Arnold & John A. Gasson, "Logotherapy and Existential Analysis." In *The Human Person* (New York: Ronald Press, 1954), p. 486.
31 Frankl, *The Doctor and the Soul*, p. 25.
32 Nathan Grossman, "The Rabbi and the Doctor of the Soul," *The Jewish Spectator*, Vol. 34 (1969), p. 11.
33 Joseph B. Fabry, *The Pursuit of Meaning: Logotherapy Applied to Life* (Boston: Beacon Press, 1968), p. 182.
34 Frankl, *Comments of Dr. Viktor E. Frankl on Logotherapy and the Talmud*, p. 4.
35 *Ibid.*, pp. 4-5.
36 Reuven P. Bulka, "The Ecumenical Ingredient in Logotherapy," *Journal of Ecumenical Studies*, Vol. 11 (1974), p. 23.
37 Donald F. Tweedie, *Logotherapy and the Christian Faith: An Evaluation of Frankl's Existential Approach to Psychotherapy* (Grand Rapids, Michigan: Baker Book House, 1965), p. 34.
38 Bulka, "The Ecumenical Ingredient in Logotherapy," *op. cit.*, p. 23.

SECTION 3
CHAPTER V
LOGOTHERAPY: ITS RELEVANCE FOR JEWISH THOUGHT

1 Talmud, *Shabbath* 153a.
2 *Ecclesiastes Rabbah* 1:13.
3 Talmud, *Erubin* 13b.
4 Viktor E. Frankl, *Die Psychotherapie in der Praxis* (Vienna: Franz Deuticke, 1947).

⁵ Talmud, *Aboth* 5:26.
⁶ Talmud, *Abodah Zarah* 10b.
⁷ Talmud, *Aboth* 2:1.
⁸ *Ecclesiastes Rabbah* 7:1.

CHAPTER VI
LOGOTHERAPY AND TALMUDIC JUDAISM

¹ Viktor E. Frankl, "The Philosophical Foundations of Logotherapy." In Erwin W. Straus (Ed.), *Phenomenology: Pure and Applied* (Pittsburgh: Duquesne University Press, 1964), p. 54.
² Frankl, *Man's Search for Meaning: An Introduction to Logotherapy* (New York: Washington Square Press, 1963), p. 154.
³ *Ibid.*, pp. 131-132.
⁴ Frankl, *Three Lectures*, Transcription of a Tape Printed as a Manuscript (Brandeis, California: Brandeis Institute, 1966), Lecture I, p. 1.
⁵ Frankl, "The Will to Meaning," *Journal of Pastoral Care*, Vol. 12 (1958), p. 87.
⁶ Frankl, "The Philosophical Foundations of Logotherapy," *op. cit.*, p. 54.
⁷ Talmud, *Aboth* 3:15.
⁸ Frankl, "The Philosophical Foundations of Logotherapy," *op. cit.*, p. 47.
⁹ *Ecclesiastes Rabbah* 1:13.
¹⁰ Frankl, "The Philosophical Foundations of Logotherapy," *op. cit.*, p. 48.
¹¹ Talmud, *Erubin* 13b.
¹² Frankl, "Self-Transcendence as a Human Phenomenon," *Journal of Humanistic Psychology*, Vol. 6 (1966), p. 100.
¹³ Talmud, *Aboth* 2:12.
¹⁴ Frankl, *The Doctor and the Soul: From Psychotherapy to Logotherapy* (New York: Bantam Books, 1967), p. xii.
¹⁵ Frankl, *Three Lectures*, lecture I, pp. 15-16.
¹⁶ Talmud, *Berakoth* 54a.
¹⁷ Frankl, *The Doctor and the Soul*, p. xii.
¹⁸ Talmud, *Ta'anith* 8a.
¹⁹ Frankl, *The Doctor and the Soul*, pp. 8-9.
²⁰ Talmud, *Abodah Zarah* 10b.
²¹ Frankl, *Man's Search for Meaning*, p. 175.
²² Talmud, *Aboth* 1:14.
²³ Frankl, *The Will to Meaning: Foundations and Applications of Logotherapy* (New York: World Publishing Co., 1969), p. 55.
²⁴ Talmud, *Aboth* 2:16.
²⁵ Frankl, *The Doctor and the Soul*, p. 60.
²⁶ Talmud, *Sanhedrin* 37a.
²⁷ Frankl, *Psychotherapy and Existentialism: Selected Papers on Logotherapy* (New York: Simon & Schuster, 1968), pp. 124-125.
²⁸ Talmud, *Kethuboth* 59b.

²⁹ Talmud, *Makkoth* 23b.
³⁰ Talmud, *Aboth* 5:16.
³¹ Frankl, *Psychotherapy and Existentialism*, pp. 30-31.
³² Frankl, "Time and Responsibility," *Existential Psychiatry*, Vol. 1 (1966), pp. 365-366.
³³ *Ecclesiastes* 7:1.
³⁴ *Tanhuma*, Vayakhel 1; *Ecclesiastes Rabbah* 7:1.
³⁵ Talmud, *Erubin* 13b.
³⁶ Talmud, *Tamid* 32a.
³⁷ Talmud, *Yebamoth* 63a.
³⁸ Frankl, *The Will to Meaning*, p. 109.

CHAPTER VII
LOGOTHERAPY AND JUDAISM

¹ Earl A. Grollman, "The Logotherapy of Viktor E. Frankl," *Judaism*, Vol. 14 (1965), p. 24.
² Viktor E. Frankl, *Comments of Dr. Viktor E. Frankl on Logotherapy and the Talmud* (San Diego: Logotherapy Institute of United States International University, 1970), p. 16.
³ *Ibid.*
⁴ Grollman, *op. cit.*, p. 24.
⁵ Viktor E. Frankl, *The Doctor and the Soul: From Psychotherapy to Logotherapy* (New York: Bantam Books, 1967), pp. ix-x.
⁶ Frankl, *Man's Search for Meaning: An Introduction to Logotherapy* (New York: Washington Square Press, 1963), p. 154.
⁷ Joseph B. Fabry, *The Pursuit of Meaning: Logotherapy Applied to Life* (Boston: Beacon Press, 1968), p. 17.
⁸ Frankl, *The Doctor and the Soul*, p. xvi.
⁹ Frankl, "Basic Concepts of Logotherapy," *Journal of Existential Psychiatry*, Vol. 3 (1962), p. 112.
¹⁰ Frankl, *The Doctor and the Soul*, p. xvii.
¹¹ *Ibid.*
¹² *Ibid.*
¹³ *Ibid.*, p. 61.
¹⁴ Frankl, "The Philosophical Foundations of Logotherapy." In Erwin W. Straus (Ed.), *Phenomenology: Pure and Applied* (Pittsburgh: Duquesne University Press, 1964), p. 43.
¹⁵ Sigmund Freud, quoted by Frankl, *The Doctor and the Soul*, p. xvii.
¹⁶ *Ibid.*
¹⁷ *Ibid.*
¹⁸ *Genesis* 5:1.
¹⁹ Talmud, *Aboth* 3:15.
²⁰ Talmud, *Berakoth* 33b.
²¹ Talmud, *Shabbath* 156a.
²² Frankl, "The Philosophical Foundations of Logotherapy," *op. cit.*, p. 47.
²³ *Ibid.*, p. 48.
²⁴ Frankl, *Man's Search for Meaning*, p. 175.

²⁵ Norman Salit, "Judaism and Psychotherapy." In Abraham Burstein (Ed.), *The Worlds of Norman Salit* (New York: Bloch Publishing, 1966), p. 292.
²⁶ *Ecclesiastes Rabbah* 1:13.
²⁷ Talmud, *Sanhedrin* 99b.
²⁸ *Ibid.*
²⁹ Richard L. Rubenstein, *The Religious Imagination: A Study in Psychoanalysis and Jewish Theology* (Boston: Beacon Press, 1971), p. 177.
³⁰ Talmud, *Aboth* 1:14.
³¹ Frankl, *The Will to Meaning: Foundations and Applications of Logotherapy* (New York: The World Publishing Co., 1968), p. 55.
³² Talmud, *Aboth* 4:5.
³³ Frankl, "Self-Transcendence as a Human Phenomenon," *Journal of Humanistic Psychology*, Vol. 6 (1966), p. 100.
³⁴ Frankl, "The Spiritual Dimension in Existential Analysis and Logotherapy," *Journal of Individual Psychology*, Vol. 15 (1959), p. 158.
³⁵ Frankl, *Psychotherapy and Existentialism: Selected Papers on Logotherapy* (New York: Simon and Schuster, 1968), p. 12.
³⁶ Frankl, *The Doctor and the Soul*, p. xii.
³⁷ *Ibid.*, p. 53.
³⁸ Talmud, *Berakoth* 5a.
³⁹ *Deuteronomy* 29:10.
⁴⁰ Talmud, *Aboth* 2:12.
⁴¹ Frankl. *Three Lectures.* Transcription of a Tape Printed as a Manuscript (Brandeis, California: Brandeis Institute, 1966), Lecture I, pp. 15-16.
⁴² Talmud, *Sanhedrin* 101a.
⁴³ Talmud, *Ta'anit* 8a.
⁴⁴ Talmud, *Aboth* 3:15.
⁴⁵ Talmud, *Abodah Zarah* 10b.
⁴⁶ Salit, *op. cit.*, p. 307.

SECTION 4
CHAPTER VIII
REFLECTIONS ON PAST AND FUTURE

¹ Talmud, *Sotah* 3a.
² Talmud, *Berakoth* 19a.
³ Talmud, *Kiddushin* 40b.
⁴ Viktor E. Frankl, *The Doctor and the Soul: From Psychotherapy to Logotherapy* (New York: Bantam Books, 1967), p. 80.
⁵ Frankl, *Psychotherapy and Existentialism: Selected Papers on Logotherapy* (New York: Simon and Schuster, 1968), pp. 30-31.
⁶ Frankl, "Time and Responsibility," *Existential Psychiatry*, Vol. 1 (1966), pp. 365-366.
⁷ *Tanhuma*, Vayakhel 1; *Ecclesiastes Rabbah* 7:1.
⁸ Frankl, *Psychotherapy and Existentialism*, p. 31.
⁹ *Ibid.*, p. 32.
¹⁰ Frankl, "Time and Responsibility," *op. cit.*, p. 363.

¹¹ Frankl, *The Will to Meaning: Foundations and Applications of Logotherapy* (New York: World Publishing Co., 1969), pp. 150-151.
¹² Frankl, *Man's Search for Meaning: An Introduction to Logotherapy* (New York: Washington Square Press, 1963), p. 187.
¹³ Frankl, *The Doctor and the Soul*, pp. 25-26.

CHAPTER IX
DEATH IN LIFE

¹ Talmud, *Yoma* 85b.
² Maimonides, *The Foundations of Torah* 5:4.
³ *Genesis Rabbah* 9:5.
⁴ Talmud, *Berakoth* 10a.
⁵ Talmud, *Aboth* 3:1.
⁶ *Ecclesiastes Rabbah* 7:9.
⁷ Talmud, *Shabbath* 152a.
⁸ Talmud, *Tamid* 32a.
⁹ *Ecclesiastes Rabbah* 8:17.
¹⁰ Viktor E. Frankl, *Man's Search for Meaning: An Introduction to Logotherapy* (New York: Washington Square Press, 1963), p. 154.
¹¹ *Ibid.*, p. 106.
¹² *Ibid.*, pp. 131-132.
¹³ Frankl, *Psychotherapy and Existentialism: Selected Papers on Logotherapy* (New York: Simon and Schuster, 1968), p. 30.
¹⁴ Frankl, *The Doctor and the Soul: From Psychotherapy to Logotherapy* (New York: Bantam Books, 1967), p. 52.
¹⁵ Frankl, *Psychotherapy and Existentialism*, p. 30.
¹⁶ Frankl, *Man's Search for Meaning*, p. 191.
¹⁷ Frankl, "Time and Responsibility," *Existential Psychiatry*, Vol. 1 (1966), p. 365.
¹⁸ *Ibid.*
¹⁹ Frankl, *The Doctor and the Soul*, p. 52.
²⁰ Elisabeth Kübler-Ross, *On Death and Dying* (New York: Macmillan, 1970), pp. 8-9.
²¹ Frankl, *The Doctor and the Soul*, p. 37.
²² *Ibid.*
²³ Herman Feifel, "The Problem of Death." In Hendrik M. Ruitenbeek (Ed.), *Death: Interpretations* (New York: Dell Publishing Co., 1969), p. 129.
²⁴ Frankl, *Psychotherapy and Existentialism*, p. 47.
²⁵ *Ibid.*, p. 36.

SECTION 5
CHAPTER X
LOGOTHERAPY AND THE TALMUD ON SUFFERING

¹ Viktor E. Frankl, *Man's Search for Meaning: An Introduction to Logotherapy* (New York: Washington Square Press, 1963), p. 154.
² Talmud, *Arakin* 16b.
³ Frankl, *Man's Search for Meaning*, p. 106.

⁴ Frankl, *The Doctor and the Soul: From Psychotherapy to Logotherapy* (New York: Bantam Books, 1967), p. xii.
⁵ Frankl, *Psychotherapy and Existentialism: Selected Papers on Logotherapy* (New York: Simon and Schuster, 1968), p. 56.
⁶ Frankl, "The Will to Meaning," *Journal of Pastoral Care*, Vol. 12 (1958), p. 86.
⁷ Frankl, *Man's Search for Meaning*, p. 115.
⁸ *Ibid.*, p. 183.
⁹ Frankl, *The Doctor and the Soul*, p. 89.
¹⁰ Frankl, *Psychotherapy and Existentialism*, pp. 15-16.
¹¹ Frankl, *The Doctor and the Soul*, p. 91.
¹² *Ecclesiastes Rabbah* 1:39.
¹³ Frankl, "Religion and Existential Psychotherapy," *Gordon Review*, Vol. 6 (1961), p. 8.
¹⁴ Frankl, "Logos and Existence in Psychotherapy," *American Journal of Psychotherapy*, Vol. 7 (1953). pp. 12-13.
¹⁵ *Ibid.*, p. 12.
¹⁶ Frankl, *The Doctor and the Soul*, p. 88.
¹⁷ Frankl, *The Will to Meaning: Foundations and Applications of Logotherapy* (New York: World Publishing Co., 1969), p. 74.
¹⁸ Frankl, *Man's Search for Meaning*, p. 13.
¹⁹ Frankl, *Comments of Dr. Viktor E. Frankl on Logotherapy and the Talmud* (San Diego: Logotherapy Institute of United States International University, 1970), pp. 6-7.
²⁰ Frankl, *Man's Search for Meaning*, p. 187.
²¹ Frankl, *The Doctor and the Soul*, p. 183.
²² Frankl, *The Will to Meaning*, p. 140.
²³ Frankl, *The Unconscious God: Psychotherapy and Theology* (New York: Simon and Schuster, 1975), p. 72.
²⁴ Frankl, *Psychotherapy and Existentialism*, pp. 92-93.
²⁵ *Ibid.*, pp. 93-94.
²⁶ *Deuteronomy* 6:5.
²⁷ Talmud, *Berakoth* 61b.
²⁸ Talmud, *Sanhedrin* 101a.
²⁹ Talmud, *Berakoth* 5a.
³⁰ *Tanchuma*, Tetze 3.

CHAPTER XI
LOGOTHERAPY AS A RESPONSE TO THE HOLOCAUST

¹ Viktor E. Frankl, *Man's Search for Meaning: An Introduction to Logotherapy* (New York: Washington Square Press, 1963), pp. 3-148.
² Irving Halperin, *Messengers from the Dead: Literature of the Holocaust* (Philadelphia: Westminster Press, no date), p. 32.
³ Talmud, *Kiddushin* 40b.
⁴ Viktor E. Frankl, "The Philosophical Foundations of Logotherapy." In Erwin W. Straus (Ed.), *Phenomenology: Pure and Applied* (Pittsburgh: Duquesne University Press, 1964), p. 55.
⁵ Talmud, *Berakoth* 61b.

SECTION 6
CHAPTER XII
THE MEANING OF LOVE

[1] Viktor E. Frankl, *Man's Search for Meaning: An Introduction to Logotherapy* (New York: Washington Square Press, 1963), p. 154.
[2] Frankl, "The Philosophical Foundations of Logotherapy." In Erwin W. Straus (Ed.), *Phenomenology: Pure and Applied* (Pittsburgh: Duquesne University Press, 1964), p. 43.
[3] Frankl, *The Doctor and the Soul: From Psychotherapy to Logotherapy* (New York: Bantam Books, 1967), p. 108.
[4] *Ibid.*, pp. 106-107.
[5] *Ibid.*, p. 107.
[6] Frankl, *Man's Search for Meaning*, pp. 58-59.
[7] Frankl, "The Task of Education in an Age of Meaninglessness." In Sidney S. Letter (Ed.), *New Prospects for the Small Liberal Arts College* (New York: Teachers College Press, 1968), p. 44.
[8] Frankl, *The Doctor and the Soul*, p. 117.
[9] Frankl, "Self-transcendence as a Human Phenomenon," *Journal of Humanistic Psychology*, Vol. 6 (1966), p. 101.
[10] Frankl, *The Doctor and the Soul*, pp. 112-113.
[11] *Ibid.*, p. 123.
[12] *Ibid.*, p. 115.
[13] Frankl, *The Unconscious God: Psychotherapy and Theology* (New York: Simon and Schuster, 1975), pp. 131-132.
[14] *Ibid.*, p. 83.
[15] *Ibid.*, p. 84.
[16] Frankl, *The Will to Meaning: Foundations and Applications of Logotherapy* (New York: World Publishing Company, 1969), p. 8.
[17] Frankl, "The Depersonalization of Sex," *Synthesis* Vol. 1 (1974), p. 10.
[18] Frankl, *Man's Search for Meaning*, pp. 194-195.
[19] William S. Sahakian & Barbara Jacquelyn Sahakian, "Logotherapy as a Personality Theory," *The Israel Annals of Psychiatry and Related Disciplines*, Vol. 10 (1972), pp. 239-240.
[20] Robert S. Weiss, *Marital Separation* (New York: Basic Books, 1975), p. 8.
[21] *Ibid.*, p. 10.
[22] Gordon W. Allport, "Comments on Earlier Chapters." In Rollo May (Ed.), *Existential Psychology* (New York: Random House, 1961), p. 97.

CHAPTER XIII
THE WORK SITUATION

[1] Viktor E. Frankl, *The Doctor and the Soul: From Psychotherapy to Logotherapy* (New York: Bantam Books, 1967), p. 154.
[2] Frankl, *Psychotherapy and Existentialism: Selected Papers on Logotherapy* (New York: Simon and Schuster, 1968), p. 82.

[3] Frankl, *The Doctor and the Soul*, p. 105.
[4] Talmud, *Aboth* 2:16.
[5] Frankl, *The Doctor and the Soul*, p. 94.
[6] *Ibid.*, pp. 44-45.
[7] *Ibid.*, p. 45.
[8] *Ibid.*, p. 34.
[9] *Ibid.*, p. 49.
[10] Frankl, *The Unconscious God: Psychotherapy and Theology* (New York: Simon and Schuster, 1975), p. 84.
[11] Talmud, *Abodah Zarah* 10b.
[12] Frankl, "The Search for Meaning," *Saturday Review*, September 18, 1958, p. 20.
[13] Frankl, *The Doctor and the Soul*, p. 43.
[14] *Ibid.*, p. 99.
[15] *Ibid.*, p. 95.
[16] *Ibid.*, pp.8-9.
[17] *Ibid.*, p. 9.
[18] *Ibid.*, p. 96.
[19] Frankl, *Man's Search for Meaning: An Introduction to Logotherapy* (New York: Washington Square Spress, 1963), p. 162.
[20] Frankl, *The Doctor and the Soul*, pp. 96-97.
[21] Frankl, *Psychotherapy and Existentialism*, p. 6.
[22] Frankl, *The Will to Meaning: Foundations and Applications of Logotherapy* (New York: World Publishing Co., 1969), pp. 96-97.
[23] Frankl, *The Doctor and the Soul*, p. 97.
[24] Talmud, *Kethuboth* 59b.
[25] Frankl, *The Doctor and the Soul*, p. 99.
[26] *Ibid.*, p. 47.
[27] Talmud, *Shabbath* 30b.
[28] Talmud, *Sanhedrin* 99b.
[29] Talmud, *Aboth* 2:16.
[30] *Ibid.*, 2:15.
[31] *Ibid.*, 2:7.
[32] Talmud, *Baba Mezia* 42a.
[33] Frankl, *The Will to Meaning*, p. 97.
[34] Talmud, *Nedarim* 41a.
[35] Talmud, *Aboth* 6:4.
[36] *Ibid.*, 2:12.

SECTION 7
CHAPTER XIV
HASIDISM AND LOGOTHERAPY

[1] Louis I. Newman, *The Hasidic Anthology: Tales and Teachings of the Hasidim* (New York: Schoken Books, 1963).
[2] Viktor E. Frankl, *Three Lectures*. Transcription of a Tape Printed as a Manuscript (Brandeis, California: Brandeis Institute, 1966).
[3] Frankl, *The Unconscious God: Psychotherapy and Theology* (New York: Simon and Schuster, 1975), p. 84.
[4] *Ibid.*, p. 124.

[5] Frankl, *Lecture given at the Inauguration of the Frankl Library and Memorabilia* (Berkeley, California: Graduate Theological Union, Feb. 12, 1977).

[6] *Ibid.*

[7] Frankl, *The Unheard Cry for Meaning: Psychotherapy and Humanism* (New York: Simon and Schuster, 1978), p. 112.

[8] *Ibid.*

[9] Frankl, *Lecture given at the Inauguration of the Frankl Library and Memorabilia.*

About the Author

Reuven P. Bulka received ordination from Rabbi Jacob Joseph Rabbinical Seminary in 1965 and a Ph.D. in Logotherapy from the University of Ottawa in 1971. He has been rabbi of Congregation Machzikei Hadas in Ottawa since 1967, and is the founding editor of the *Journal of Psychology and Judaism*, published since 1976. Host of the weekly TV series "In Our Hands" and the radio call-in program "Religion on the Air," he is also chaplain of the Dominion Command of the Royal Canadian Legion, President of the International Rabbinic Forum of Keren HaYesod, Chairman of the Rabbinic Cabinet for State of Israel Bonds in Canada, Chairman of the Religious and Inter-Religious Affairs Committee of Canadian Jewish Congress, and Chairman of the Religious Advisory Committee for United Way of Ottawa-Carlton. He is the author or editor of thirty books and 100 articles on psychology- and Judaism-related themes, and his books are syndicated in various national newspapers.